Key Issues in Critical and Cultural Theory

Key Issues in Critical and Cultural Theory

Kate McGowan

Open University Press

Open University Press
McGraw-Hill Education
McGraw-Hill House
Shoppenhangers Road
Maidenhead
Berkshire
England
SL6 2QL

email: enquiries@openup.co.uk
world wide web: www.openup.co.uk

and Two Penn Plaza, New York, NY 10121–2289, USA

First published 2007

A catalogue record of this book is available from the British Library

ISBN-10: 0335 218 032 (pb)
0335 218 040 (hb)

ISBN-13: 9780 335 035 (pb)
9780 335 218 042 (hb)

Library of Congress Cataloguing-in-Publication Data
CIP data applied for

Typeset by YHT Ltd, London
Printed in Poland by OzGraf S.A.
www.polskabook.pl

The McGraw·Hill Companies

Contents

Acknowledgements

While to acknowledge the debt to previous writings and ideas is inevitably to risk the curtailment of the potentially infinite, I should like to thank Margaret Beetham, Lucy Burke, Simon Malpas, Arthur McGowan, Shafqat Nasir, Jacqueline Roy and Berthold Schoene, for their engagement in various ways with the process of thinking things through. In addition, I also owe a genuine debt of gratitude to all the students at Manchester Metropolitan University, past and present, who have in some ways shaped the terms of the approach to the concept of 'issues' in critical theory. Their tireless excitement for ideas and the relentless unpredictability of their questions are invaluable. As is customary now, I should also point out that what follows is in no way the fault of those mentioned above.

I should also like to thank the publishers and editors for their patience, Chris Cudmore for his enthusiasm and support, and the readers whose suggestions at a formative stage worked to shape the project in positive ways.

Finally, special thanks go to Shafqat Nasir for putting up with the neurosis that is the condition for writing for some, and to my Dad, whose willingness to debate the illogicality of the taken for granted in culture, I still find amazing.

Introduction

Man uses electric underpants 'to feign heart attack'
www.guardian.co.uk

In October 1999, a man is alleged to have wired a domestic iron to give himself an electric shock and then used an 'amps-in-his-pants' device to convince a hospital heart monitor that he had had a heart attack and that his heart was subsequently beating irregularly. His scheme was uncovered, by hospital staff, and his case came to court on 4 July 2005. It was reported first on *The Guardian* newspaper website early on 5 July 2005, under the heading quoted above, and then in *The Guardian* newspaper with the transmuted title of 'Man used electric underpants "to fake heart attack"' later the same day. The man's purpose in all of this was to sue the manufacturers of the product for £300,000 damages (*Guardian* 2005: 6).

I find this story fascinating, partly because it has a Warner Brothers twist to it where Wile E. Coyote never gets the results he so desperately wants, and partly because it works at so many levels as an index of cultural consciousness not limited to the twenty-first century. It is at once a story of the enterprise of 'the little guy' in the face of the big corporations, and at the same time one of the hapless certainty of the **other**, demonstrating a popular thirst for the strange and bizarre which confirms the 'normality' of its readers. It's also fascinating as an example of culture's obsession with the uneasy boundaries between what it thinks of as 'real', or 'authentic', and that which distinguishes that real in the form of the 'not real'. To feign is to simulate, while to fake is to copy. Simulation has the effect of producing the thing which it abolishes in order to appear in its place. Copying produces a secondary representation. That the headline slides from 'feign' to 'fake', in the move from electronic text to printed paper, suggests a further anxiety recuperated by producing a **sign** which has greater potential to arrest the uncertainty generated, albeit unconsciously, by the first. If the man faked the heart attack, then he didn't really have one and the real of the organic body can remain intact. If he feigned it, then it's more complicated, though still, of course, recuperable. The reader has to work harder with the first version than the second. Did the man have a heart attack or not? Was his self-inflicted electric shock any less real than it would have been had it come as a surprise? And, did those 'amps-in-his-pants' really fake the symptoms or actually produce the conditions necessary for a heart attack, and so produce a heart attack like any other?

By 7 July 2005, British newspapers had dropped all such seemingly frivolous reporting in the face of the bombings on the London Underground and on a number 30 bus that would subsequently become known as '7/7'. For weeks British media interest was taken up with the story of the four men who packed rucksacks full of explosives and entered various tube stations across London in the rush hour, boarded packed trains and a bus and then detonated their explosives killing themselves and others around them. What everyone seemed to want to know was, why? Even now, the questions remain: why did they do it and what does it *mean*? Apart from the obvious horror of the situation, the fascination has consistently been about why British citizens would do such a thing, and how, prior to the act, the men displayed no discernible signs of being anything other than the regular members of the collective 'us' that, allegedly, makes up British culture and society today. As images and eye witness accounts, stories of suspicion and failure to 'read the signs' correctly, proliferated in the aftermath of the day itself, the 'event' of 7 July was produced as an effect of representations which retrospectively sought to give meaning to what had, in the immediacy of the event, seemed 'senseless'.

The consequences of the events in London are, of course, far more serious than those of the case of the man with the electric underpants. At the same time, however, both display a set of concerns about **signification** and interpretation that pose particular sorts of problems for any practice of cultural criticism. These might include questions about representation – how it comes to generate meaning and how it can be said to relate, if at all, to something called the real. They might also include more detailed questions about aesthetics – how images and words function in reference to all other forms of representation which surround and precede them, but also as an effect produced in the reader or viewer of those images and words. Why, for example, are images of traumatic events reproduced over and over again? Is there some sort of mastery afforded the viewer in the anxious reiteration of representation of events which substitute for the events they supposedly 're-present'? And, what of the highly contentious terrain of pleasure – either the pleasure of the image itself or of the position afforded the viewer – of something which, while traumatic, is at least not happening to them? In turn, such questions also seem to give rise to further debates about ethics – about whether it is either ethical, or not, to depict events in culture in certain ways, or to critique the depictions that do circulate in any kind of persistently interrogative fashion. Central to competing claims over the ethics of cultural criticism is a notion of the real as a reference point of veracity or authenticity, where the relativization of analyses is supposed to come to an end in morality. But this gives rise to at least one more question in the shape of the human and its 'place' in the world of culture as a viable concept of analysis.

The London bombings have become one of the cultural texts of this century to be subjected to seemingly endless possibilities of interpretation, re-interpretation and the contested truth claims of a variety of interests. In part, the meaning of the event in this case has come to radically depend upon a relation to another event which, while sharing some of its components, also overshadows it in its supposed concentration of significance. As the swift labelling of the day of the bombings in London as '7/7' suggests, it was, almost from the start, impossible to read those events outside of a framework for making sense which had previously been established by the destruction of the twin towers of the World Trade Center, in New York, on 11 September 2001. '7/7' and '9/11' signify explicitly in relation to one another by marking a sameness which is both textual and ideological, and thus concealing the differences that might be drawn between Britain, and its political landscape, and the United States of America with its economy. It was fortunate in this respect that the men who used the explosives on the London tubes and bus chose 7 July for their actions, since the symmetry of '7/7' hides a basic grammatological difference between the British and American conventions for signifying time in terms of the Gregorian calendar. While the British are in the habit of writing the day and then the month, Americans write, and so comprehend, the month followed by the day. Thus, '7/7' in some ways conceals the difference between two understandings of historical time, while foregrounding a certain sense of sameness. However, it also marks an ambivalence, since it can be read as at once both concealing *and* revealing the difference upon which it depends.

Seemingly ubiquitous in its capacity to **signify** metaphorically and metonymically, '7/7' also asserts itself in the place of less widely analyzed events of similar consequence. Bombings in Palestine and Iraq, even in Madrid, are all too easily repressed in this respect in the formation of a supposedly 'global' threat to all democracy-loving peoples. So, '7/7' comes to mean both by virtue of its relation to something which is thereby similar, and by the **disavowal** of that which is similar, but not similar enough. In this sense, meaning is also clearly an issue of value. However, while the link to events which have preceded '7/7' works, in part, to produce the retrospective meaning of it in this way, it also eclipses it in another chain of signification which asserts yet another value: that of American political dominance. Indeed, the events of September 11 2001, in New York City, have come to dominate and to define the terms of a global **imaginary** in ways which the bombings in London could never do. As such, '9/11' is probably the most widely circulating sign in culture today.

With the saturation of the images by which '9/11' has come to be known, it is difficult to escape the challenge of reading which those images pose. From the **uncanny** shot of the second plane, which was filmed from below by a tourist video camera, to the repeated images of ordinary people running screaming from a giant cloud of smoke, '9/11' is embedded in the cultural memory of our time in particular ways. However, while these images were shot on the run, impromptu and unexpectedly, they are also, in the very instant of their production, held in reference to others which have gone before them. The shot of the plane is uncanny precisely because it is caught in an aesthetic tradition direct from Hollywood. While the shots of people running are inevitably infused by other images, particularly in this instance, the iconic image of the young girl running from the mushroom cloud of the atomic bomb deployed against civilians in Nagasaki during the Second World War. Although they are offered as 'authentic', because they are instant, these images of '9/11' also attest to the thoroughly cultural structuration of human perception, even experience, layered as both are by the operation of forms of representation which produce them. That the power of such structures persists, even when perception is not conscious of itself as such is startling, since what it reveals is the play of signification in sense-making processes, rather than the supposed **immanentism** of experience it might otherwise appear to affirm.

By foregrounding the structural and ideological dependency within which any images necessarily operate, a certain denaturalizing of what they may signify becomes possible. In the case of the saturation of the images post '9/11', this seems like an urgent task. Indeed, what accounts of the **textuality** of the apparently spontaneous representations, by which we have come to think we 'know' '9/11' can provide, is the glimpse of an alternative set of meanings already at work within them. Of course, it's perfectly possible to read the photographs of running people within a framework which eschews the cultural and political differences upon which they depend. But it is equally possible to refuse to do so and, in so doing, to resist the commonsense values which are apparently so easily affirmed there. In these terms, the values taken for granted in the circulation of these images may be disrupted and, like a spectre of its own past, the indifferent instance of America's actions in the world can be said to return to haunt it. The implications of such an observation, as subsequent cultural criticism has revelled in revealing, are vast and various.

Consider, for a moment, this one image of New York City on 11 September 2001 (Figure I.1). What is the value of understanding this image as the photographic capture of a real moment? On the one hand, it clearly *is* the capture of a moment in the instant of that moment. On the other, it is also so evidently 'staged' that it also attests to so much more than what simply 'is'. If it is the capture of a real moment, then what is captured is not the *real* of the real moment but rather its condition as always already constructed. While the trauma of the moment of an explosion is *in* the image, by virtue of the flying debris and the unusually large and close cloud of smoke, it is also at once mastered by the assertion of the signifier of Christian faith in the cross as the rock on which its Church is founded. The plume of destruction is clearly

Figure I.1 New York City, September 11 2001

Source: Photograph for *TIME* by James Nachtway/VII

arrested in the image by the sign of the cross. But, the centrality of the cross to the image has further consequences in delimiting the event it metaphorically depicts by displacing it onto the film of the camera. The cross suggests a meaning for the event caught in the encounter between Islam and Christianity upon which contemporary discussions about 'terror' rely. Erased from the field of vision, global politics and economy are instantly irrelevant to what the destruction of the twin towers of the World Trade Center is able to signify. However, returned to it, they begin to inhabit that signification in ways that produce a very different set of possibilities for what it might mean.

The image of the cross also serves to explain the image as a whole. What, after all, is 'there' in this image which secures it as an image pertaining to a particular day in a particular city? It *could* be an image of demolition in any city across the world. But, it isn't. What invests the signification possible in this photograph takes place, ironically, off stage in another set of naturalized symbols of a 'clash' between two faiths. The photograph then means by virtue of a relationship to something outside of itself which is also, paradoxically, at work within it. And, all of this in an instant of pointing a lens at an object which, photography asserts is simply 'happening'.

While this reading of the image is possible, it is clearly not an uninterested one. It involves conceptualizations of signification, referentiality, aesthetics, and the real. It also works within conceptions of ethics and of the human which are removed from common sense. But, is there any reading of any image which does not always entail such judgements? To read with the grain of the image is also, surely, to mobilize conceptual thinking, even if that thinking is not in itself foregrounded.

From the seemingly mundane report of the man with the electric underpants, to the ironic and complex representations by which the events of

September 11 and 7 July have come to be known, the issues of signifying, reading and comprehending the world inhabited by the human animal, are readily and endlessly apparent. However, the terms within which such signification, reading and comprehension may take place, have hardly been examined in the popular manifestations of them which surround us. In just these three examples, a host of issues are raised concerning meaning and interpretation which might otherwise have gone unnoticed by recourse to the platitudes of 'truth', 'experience', 'the obvious', and, worse still, 'common sense'. Of course, this is not always the case. The vested interests of the electric underpants scam are never far from the terrain of understanding the act and any subsequent decoding of it which may be performed. Similarly, the interests of the Blair Government in Britain, the Bush administration in the USA, or the democratic processes of France and Germany, as well as all of those who in varying ways oppose them, are never, in practice, far from the scene of the rhetoric and actions incited by their various deployments. And, as conspiracy narratives abound, those interests become the driving forces of supposedly clear explanations, meanings and a different sort of consensus.

Cultural criticism, on the other hand, demands a much more rigorous attention to both the mechanics and effects of such significations, the practices involved in generating readings of them, and the consequences of the meanings thus produced from them or importantly, contested within them. If it is to be more than simply a parasitic means of reiterating the sense of culture, then cultural criticism must not only be critically aware of the frameworks it utilizes, but also able to account for its practices in ways which remain open to intellectual examination and can, on that basis, also be disputed, contested and ultimately even rearranged.

Juxtaposing two stories – of a man and his underpants and two acts of terror in the twenty-first century – immediately poses a set of issues about the operation of cultural texts which must be dealt with by cultural criticism right from the start: what is its 'proper' object? Among the questions immediately raised by considering the object of cultural criticism are those concerning value. For example, does cultural criticism focus on the mundane, the glamorous, the canonical, the marginal, the popular and/or the elite? How do cultural critics decide on the status of their object? Is the mundane less significant than the spectacular, the canonical more worthy of analysis than the marginal, or vice versa? Should cultural criticism even deal in these terms and distinctions in carrying out its specific intellectual project? In short, one might come to ask again, what does cultural criticism *do* and what is it *for*?

The argument of this book is that cultural criticism offers a distinct way of engaging with culture, and the meanings generated within cultures, which matter in the world today. Without an understanding of what generates the meanings by which both the world, and we in relation to that world, come to be defined, dominant cultural meanings go uncontested in any thorough or lasting terms. It is crucial, therefore, that cultural criticism is equipped to offer much more than just dissent at the level of meaning as it appears in culture, supposedly fully formed. Rather, it must critically engage the very constitution of the possibility of meaning in the first place – how we come to know, to interpret and apparently to comprehend, anything at all. What cultural criticism must contest, then, is not only the interpretation of different texts of a culture or cultural moment, but also the very terms by which the possibility of thought itself can be manifest in relation to the concept of a text, a culture, a moment, indeed, a whole metaphysical system of being in the world. Stated like this, cultural criticism matters, because it matters to 'us'. That is, it provides frameworks within which it is possible to confront and to explore what it means to be, to think, to consider and to judge, in the world today. And, cultural criticism in this sense should be relentless.

It should encompass the texts of the everyday, the mundane and the ridiculous alongside those credited with greater depth, seriousness or value. It should attend to the meanings produced both within, and in our relation to, the texts of the culture we inhabit, whatever forms those texts may take. It should be capable of engaging critically with an event, an action, a symbol, as equally well as with a novel of great or popular literature, a Hollywood romance or avant-garde cinema, even the musical arrangements of sound from classical traditions as diverse as, say, those of Mozart, the Arctic Monkeys or Kylie Minogue. It should be capable of analyzing the specificities of textual forms for the meanings they generate and circulate. It should, of course, also be able to deal with the issues of author- and reader-ship which arise even from the designations which have, of necessity, just been drawn. Cultural criticism must, in other words, also be capable of critical engagement with the texts of critical and cultural theory themselves.

In order to do this, cultural criticism needs a set of tools with which it can perform the work which this book is suggesting it is vital to do. Without carefully constituted frameworks for thinking, cultural criticism cannot hope to intervene in any serious manner with the questions of value inherent in the culture it critiques.

Following what has been termed a '**poststructuralist**' pathway through the explosion of different theories of cultural study available today, this book makes a particular case for thinking of culture as an effect of systems of meaning rather than self-evident truths and, as such, focuses primarily on meaning as signification, difference and displacement. The issues thus addressed are issues which have arisen within, and been contested by, that stance as well as others opposed to it. Inevitably, within each of the chapters presented here, a position defined in these terms is also taken. While a range of ways of thinking is set out in the course of this study, this is not simply an objective survey of the material open to a critic of culture today. Each chapter elucidates the terrain of its subject and declares a position on it. Within this framework, these positions are never a matter of individual taste but are situated clearly within a continuous strand of thinking invested by key poststructuralist ideas. In this way, as well as charting what is at issue in critical and cultural theory today, the aim is also to distinguish and demarcate a body of knowledge in terms of the possibilities it opens up.

To this end, the book is structured into six chapters, each of which may be read individually. At the same time, the cumulative effect of reading the chapters in sequence may offer an increasingly intense engagement, not only with the issues involved, but also with the possibility that what is discussed here forms a broader confluence from which it is ultimately impossible to separate off the component parts.

Chapter 1, 'Textuality and Signification', deals explicitly with the issue of 'the text', or 'textuality', and of a cultural practice which foregrounds the process of signification itself as important to cultural criticism. This involves accounts of different theories of both, but also an argument for the possibilities opened up by such an approach for the practices of cultural criticism that may ensue. Chapter 2, 'Aesthetics', extends the discussion of the issues of text and signification by examining the ways in which both constitute signifying effects. This necessitates an exploration of theories of aesthetics, as well as an account of what can be at stake in the terms of such a discussion for the ways in which criticism thinks not only about the texts of culture, but also about culture's relation to them. This begins to foreground questions about the politics of cultural criticism. Chapter 3, 'Ethics', takes this politics seriously and looks specifically at theories of ethics, asking whether or not something like an ethics of cultural criticism might be possible. In doing so, the chapter also explores what is at stake in thinking of actions, critiques or cultural practices as either intrinsically ethical or not, in every instance of that thinking. Chapter 4, 'Alterity', extends this exploration by focusing specifically on the issue of the other, and on the mutually constitutive relation between self and other, which is always entailed in thinking through issues of 'alterity' of all kinds. Chapter 5, 'The Real', takes us into the realms of the contested conceptual space of the real on which an ethics may or may not be based. From theories of the real as a void, through those of the real as something like 'perception', to the real as that which can never be comprehended within the realms of meaning, what is at stake in different constitutions is examined. Finally, Chapter 6, 'The Inhuman', deals with an issue that can be traced within all of the others but, from which it retains a certain sort of distance, in that it can be said to distil the cumulative significance of preceding discussions within the figure of the human. Whether the human can remain at the end of this analysis is a question which, as the chapter will explore, remains very much to be seen.

Some of the ideas elaborated in the course of the discussions staged here are inevitably difficult, especially when they are encountered for the first time. While this is not exactly an introductory book – it presumes a certain familiarity at least with some of the positions discussed – particularly difficult or contentious terms will appear in the text in bold the first time they are used and are defined in a Glossary of terms at the end of the book. In addition, for those readers who wish to venture beyond the terrain of this modest work, there is also a full bibliography.

1 Textuality and Signification

- Why textuality and signification?
- The move from work to text
- The movement of signification
- Writing as iterability
- The subject as text
- The issue of textuality and signification

Why textuality and signification?

Since the critical practice advocated here is one that foregrounds the process of signification, it makes sense to begin with a detailed exploration of the concepts that inform that practice. This chapter, therefore, begins by tracing the emergence within critical thinking of the concepts of 'textuality' and 'signification' in order to demonstrate the contribution they make to debates about what cultural criticism is and what it can do. This may entail revisiting some basic theoretical principles which are already familiar. However, since the argument staged is one that relies on a precise understanding of these principles, it is just as well to be clear, from the beginning, about what they involve and why. From this understanding, the chapter moves on to explore ways in which the concepts of textuality and signification inform particular practices of cultural criticism, and to examine the issues that thinking of culture as textual effect can be said to raise.

The move from work to text

In an essay first published in French as 'De l'œuvre au texte' in 1971, but later translated into English by Stephen Heath as 'From Work to Text' in 1977, the structuralist critic Roland Barthes (1915–80) laid down some preliminary foundations for a shift in critical thinking that had been underway in France for some time. These are worth closer examination, since they demonstrate what is at issue in conceptualizations of both the work and the text, and why the move was advocated. While the translation of the title encapsulates the conceptual trajectory of Barthes' essay – the shift from thinking in terms of the work to those of the text – the earlier title acknowledges something more of the idea of Barthes' ideological project in its emphasis on the work *performed* by the text. Both are important in what results.

For Barthes, the concept of the work is unhelpful to the project of cultural criticism since it closes off both the creative possibilities of cultural study, and the capacity of that study to acknowledge the political significance of the ways in which objects of study can be said to operate. For him, the concept of the work has at least two important drawbacks – filiation and consumption. Invoking the law of copyright as a legal embodiment of the concept at hand, Barthes suggests that one problem with the concept of the work in culture is that the object becomes solidified by it. That is, it becomes explicable in terms of its status as the 'property' of the author who produced it, and is subsequently determined by what it is imagined that author intended. In this way, the concept of the work is inscribed by what Barthes calls the name of the 'father'. In the conventional way of the work, Jane Austen's *Emma* becomes explicable in terms of Jane Austen (the author), terms which might include her sensibility, her gift for a certain kind of written expression, and so on. It is conceivable within the terms marked by the concept of the work that the author might be displaced, but still the work is determined by its relation to a thing which is said to explain it. History, for example, could work conceptually just as well as the author in this respect. We might then say that the time in which Jane Austen wrote *Emma* made *Emma* possible in the way that it is now manifest to us, because of the position of women, the laws on marriage and property, and so on, that pertained at the time. Whichever way we look at it, the concept of the work, defined in these terms, determines the nature and perception of the object studied by fixing it in relation to a 'thing' which in turn explains it. It *conforms*, in other words, to the thing by which it is understood, and in that conformity both it, and any interpretation of it, are complete.

This completeness of the work gives rise to a second conceptual problem identified by Barthes, that of the work as an object of consumption. When we consume something, we eat it. That is, we take something which is fully formed and integral to itself – an apple, say – and we ingest it by taking it into ourselves in order to produce a feeling of contentment, good health, even the satisfaction of something we call hunger. But, is that really all a work, a cultural object, is? What is at issue in thinking of the work as a product of an author to be consumed by a reader who simply ingests it? One issue identified in critical thinking is that of the passivity prescribed for the reader by this model. Here, criticism is constituted simply in an act of consumption involving, at best, judgements of taste. This produces the kind of criticism with which we are probably already familiar: *Macbeth* is better than *Trainspotting* because it's more sophisticated or self-enhancing. In either case, the object remains the same, and so does the reader. We respond to what is contained in the integrity of the work as such, and simply digest it accordingly. Reading, in this sense, is like consumption because it does not involve any kind of process, either within the work or the reader, or between the work and the reader. As such, it can be argued that the concept of the work gives rise to a notion of cultural criticism as simply the parasitic task of summarizing what the work already says, or of judging that work on the basis of a knowledge of other works which can subsequently be said to be like or unlike it, according to the expert taste of the critic.

The implications of the concept of the work, then, are that it constitutes the object of study as a fixed and solid thing in its own right, over and done with at the moment the last full stop is in place, and as something which is open only to being understood in the terms which the work itself is judged to set out. This raises a whole set of issues about what constitutes the 'proper' object of cultural study, what that object can be said to do, and how we as critics, can be said to engage it.

The concept of the text, on the other hand, releases a different set of possibilities both for the constitution of cultural objects and for the subsequent understanding of their significance. For Barthes, while the concept of the work is founded on assumptions that close down the possibilities of the object as well as its study, the concept of the text opens them up in some radical ways.

In the first place, the text 'is not to be thought of as an object that can be computed' (Barthes 1990: 157). This would appear to involve three new premises which were not available to the conceptualization of the object of study as a work. These are space, time and resistance. While the space of the work is clear – it exists in a library, for example, on a shelf from which we can then take it down and ingest it – the space of the text is more open in that it is constituted as part of, and in a vital relation to, 'a methodological field' (1990: 157). Here, the space of the text is no longer its own, rather, it becomes open, multiple and shifting, according to the relation within which it might be situated at any given time. In this sense, the text of *Henry IV* performed at the Globe in the seventeenth century is not the same as the text I might have read as a student of English Literature in the twentieth century, situated as I was within a different set of knowledges and understandings to those of the audience at the Globe. Nor is it the same as the text that I might subsequently watch on television or in the cinema – especially in the different moment of the 'now' within which I write this example, and which is largely characterized by continual discussion in the media about suicide bomb attacks around the world. What changes in this concept of the space of the text is the notion that the meaning of the text, what I understand when I read it, will not be entirely tied to the text itself as constituted in the words on the page. Implicit here is a notion of the text as in some way *un*-finished at the moment of the final full stop. Rather, it is now open to the vagaries of time, in that what it signifies will be open to change in the shifting relations among the object, the world and the **subject**, located in that world in space and time, which performs the reading of it. It will also, significantly, be changed by a conceptual approach to it which does not take meaning for granted and so is not limited by the most obvious interpretations offered by the work itself. The text, unfinished, incomplete even to itself, opens up another kind of space: that of resistance. The score of 'Wonderwall' (1995), for example, released from its assumed determined relation to either the Gallagher brothers and all that we 'know' of their exploits, or to Burnage and all we know of what that signifies as a particular district of Manchester, becomes readable in terms of those elements which resist as well as confirm a sensible reading of it as such.[1] The reading thus produced, is a resistant reading – it comes from a methodological field which conceives of the text as open – but it also constitutes the text as a dissonant space, a space within which its significations do not necessarily cohere.

For this to be the case, the text cannot be understood as an entity closed and integral to itself. What the concept of the text offers in this sense, then, is the object as incomplete to itself and subsequently opened up to the possibilities yet to come for itself, in the interactive process of reading. This concept of the text also puts the act of reading into process, since it becomes less a moment of consumption and more an ongoing process of production, which itself is open to new possibilities as yet unanticipated.

If the text cannot be computed, then it can no longer be explained as derived from a single source either. This opens up the possibility that the text does not exist in isolation – it may well refer to other writings, or to the rules of a genre of writing – and that the meanings to which it may be said to give rise are not determined in relation to a single, coherent, point. It becomes perfectly possible in this sense to see the ways in which a text like *Emma* might well contain elements of writing which suggest conformity to the social mores of either its author or its time, but also *and at the same time*, elements of writing which resist these things, and so work against the grain of the obvious message of the text. This model of the text as always, already internally conflicted, allows the production of contradiction and resistance to ideas – about women, about marriage or about class – which may otherwise be taken for granted as obvious, natural or true. There might even be elements of the text, conceived of in these terms, which explicitly go against the rules of writing itself. There may be elements of a novel, for example, which, while being a novel in a classically agreed sense, might also work against that – including, say, fragments of writing which follow the conventions of poetry, the interjection of visual images, even nonsense. The text may, while operating largely within the bounds of the rules of English grammar, contain, perhaps even foreground, the breaking of those rules. *Alice's Adventures in*

Wonderland, with its attention to the logic and hence illogical possibilities of language, is a text which does just that:

> 'Of course not,' said the Mock Turtle. 'Why, if a fish came to *me*, and told me he was going a journey, I should say "With what porpoise?"'
>
> 'Don't you mean "purpose"?' said Alice.
>
> 'I mean what I say,' the Mock Turtle replied, in an offended tone.
> (Carroll 2000: 109)

Another example might be *Ulysses*, where language itself is fragmented, disordered and put out of joint, in an effort to foreground what is at stake in the process of meaning making. A series of sentences like, 'Golly, whatten tunket's yon guy in the mackintosh? Dusty Rhodes. Peep at his wearables. By mighty!' (Joyce 1982: 424) seems as much to refer to itself as a process of signification as it does to anything that might, therefore, be signified separately by it.

In both cases, to solidify these writings would also be to reduce their meaning by closing off the multiplicities to which their self-referential practice points. Thought of as works, *Alice's Adventures in Wonderland* and *Ulysses* remain within the confines of sense. Thought of as texts, they come not only to signify in multiple and shifting ways, but also to signify something more about the nature of signification itself. In addition, rather than passively consuming the work, the reader is invited to actively engage in the process of meaning making which the texts themselves explore.

So, the concept of the text as Barthes defines it allows for the multiplicity of signification – its contradictions, ambiguities and mistakes – to be foregrounded. Here, the hesitancy of aspects of the text which would, by necessity, have been repressed in the concept of the work may be liberated from it. In addition, the meanings read from the text will always be relational – to themselves in the space of the text, in the reading of the text, and in the time of the text constituted in the act of reading.

While texts are, for Barthes, *always* 'paradoxical', 'irreducibly plural', and 'woven entirely with citations, references, echoes, cultural languages ... which cut across it through and through in a vast stereophony' (1990: 160), they are by necessity also always constitutable in such terms because they are always in relation to *signification*. If the text can be approached in relation to the sign, then the text is opened to the movement of the sign that constitutes signification. In this way, any utterance, any instance of writing, indeed, any form of representation, becomes subject to the internal rules of the system which generates it. In one sense, conceiving of the text as a signifying space entails an approach to the text as an alienated object, governed not by intent or design, but rather by the processes of signification which are to a large extent beyond its control. In another sense, constituted by the process of signification, the text ceases to be an integral space and becomes instead an *effect* of the process that signifying is. Read as signification, the textuality of the text is foregrounded.

The movement of signification

Barthes' reference to the concept of the sign in 1977 is a reference to the work of the Swiss linguist, Ferdinand de Saussure (1857–1913), on whose work he draws. The work of Saussure has been significant in the development of cultural criticism through the twentieth century and continues to exert an influence on contemporary thinking, though it has faded somewhat as an area of interest in its own right. Despite this, the *Course in General Linguistics* (1966) remains vital since it marks a massive shift not only in the way we are able to think about language, but also the ways in which we are subsequently able to conceive of ourselves as subjects of and to language, and of reality as subject of and to the process of signification which representation then becomes.[2]

Among the concepts which Saussure's work provides to critical thinking is that of language as a system of signs. This rather mundane-sounding proposition has far-reaching consequences. It shifts the thinking of language as merely descriptive (a set of names for things) into the realm of thinking of language as constitutive of those things. Here, language as a system of signs can now be understood to generate the very things it was once said merely to grasp.

Language works in this respect because of what it does. No longer either innate or natural, language is acquired by human animals in a process of cultural inculcation which determines, or *structures*, their capacity to think within its terms.[3] It does this by dividing and associating. In the first instance, language divides the continua of thought and sound. Prior to language, humans may have the capacity for thought and sound, but that capacity is as yet unstructured. Babies may gurgle, but they don't yet have language (Latin *infans*: without language); they may have sensation, but they must learn to think:

> To prove that language is only a system of pure values, it is enough to consider the two elements involved in its functioning: ideas and sounds.
>
> Psychologically our thought – apart from its expression in words – is only a shapeless and indistinct mass. Philosophers and linguists have always agreed in recognizing that without the help of signs we

> would be unable to make a clear-cut, consistent distinction between two ideas. Without language, thought is a vast uncharted nebula. There are no pre-existing ideas, and nothing is distinct before the appearance of language.
>
> Against this floating realm of thought, would sounds themselves yield any predelimited entities? No more so than ideas.
>
> (de Saussure 1966: 111–12)

So, both thought and sound for Saussure exist as continua which he conceives of as 'waves' (Figure 1.1).

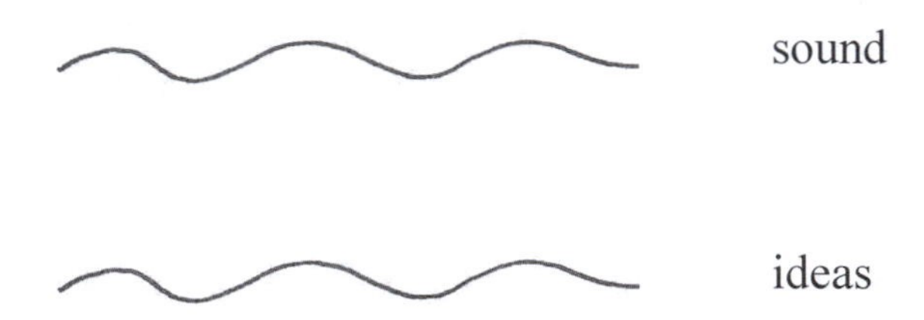

Figure 1.1 Sound and thought represented as waves

Language structures these continua by cutting across them and thus instituting divisions which are in an important sense arbitrary.[4] Sound thus becomes, in the first instance, phonetic – we learn to distinguish the acceptable bits of sound that the cutting of language makes on the continuum, and to distinguish those bits from those which are *not* acceptable in the terms of the language we acquire. Blowing raspberries is, for example, currently to be discouraged in English babies intent on signifying in any seriously meaningful way. This is an arbitrary process, since what counts as 'acceptable' varies from language to language. What is important is that the language community into which we are inducted by this process agrees on the assignment of *value*. As language structures sound, so it also structures thought. On the range of the continuum of thought, language makes cuts which divide it by marking the difference of one space between cuts to that of another. On a spectrum of colour, for example, it is possible for the concept of 'orange' to emerge by virtue of a relationship of difference to a concept of 'red' which comes before it and a concept of 'yellow' which follows. What would constitute the concept 'orange' in the absence of 'red' would be different, but it would still be produced in a differential relation. Perhaps the range of what constitutes 'orange' with 'red' would be contracted to produce another prior category by which 'orange' could be defined. Either way, what constitutes 'orange' is not intrinsic to it but can and will change according to the relations of difference from which it comes. Thus, thought becomes conceptual in that it is generated by the system of differentiating which language, understood in these terms, is.

Having differentiated in these ways, language also serves to forge associations.[5] Cutting across the continua of sound and thought, language links

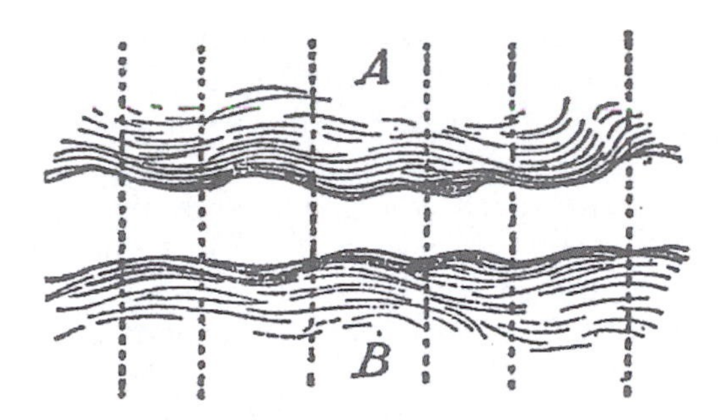

Figure 1.2 Saussure's wave diagram

together the divisions it makes (Figure 1.2).
The continuum A is divided by the vertical line (language) but also linked by it to a division on continuum B, to which it is then associated by the line itself. The work of cutting which produces the divisions then also forges the associations. Again, this is in an important sense arbitrary, since where cuts and associations are made will radically depend only on the terms of the language system which performs them. But it is also communal, or social, since the terms of a language system are shared within a language group or culture. This goes a long way to accounting for cultural difference, as simply that: difference. While the systematic process is universal, the terms of that process are particular.

The association of acoustic and conceptual bits emerging from the divisions of these two continua takes place within the sign. Understood in this way, the sign is no longer referential. That is, it is not a sign of something outside of itself which it merely represents, but rather an arbitrary association made by and within the system which generates it. Famously, the sign is composed of the signifier and the signified, where the signifier is the acoustic, or visual, effect of the cut on the continuum of sound, and the signified, the conceptual effect of the cut on the continuum of thought. Associated by language, they form the sign. In order to produce the sign 'cat', for example, I must combine the phonetic sounds 'c-a-t' with the conceptual category of a small, furry, whiskered, domestic animal distinguished from a range of possible animals organized by a division between those I eat and those I pet.

Signs, then, are not only systematic. They are, as a result of the system, an effect of both difference and association which is specific to a particular language culture. One implication of this, as noted earlier, is that signs are no longer referential. They cannot, by virtue of being signs, refer to anything outside of themselves which is not itself also an effect of the system which generates them. Signs refer, then, only to other signs, and that process of referral is what constitutes signification as a movement in both space and time.

Signification, understood as a process of referral of signs, can no longer be conceived of as static, fixed, or whole to itself, but rather becomes, open, fluid and self-referential. And, it is *this* idea of signification which Barthes borrows from Saussure for his conceptualization of the text as '*always* "paradoxical"' ... woven entirely with citations, reference echoes, cultural languages' (1990: 158, 160). Whenever we refer to signification in cultural criticism, the weight of this analysis inevitably bears upon it.

If we return momentarily to the example of the photograph which stands as a representation of '9/11' cited in the Introduction (Figure I.1), some of the consequences of a theory of signification can be read from it. Immediately, we are moved to approach the text by asking what it signifies. We might jump to the end of the process by suggesting that it signifies the transcendent power of the Christian faith to arrest the resistance to that faith which Islam is imagined to be, thus offering a meaning for '9/11' which is resolute. But we arrive at such a meaning only by virtue of an understanding of signification as the relational movement of different signs in the assemblage of the image. On the basis of this, the image can no longer be thought of as authentic, but rather as an effect of the staging of signification in relation to cultural value, even in the instant of the click of the camera shutter. Freed from the determination of the notion of experience – of either the photographer or the viewer of the photograph – the text is also opened to dissent and contestation. We might, for example, read it as the failure of signification, or of signs to stay where they are put. The cross, in this reading, may well seem resolute, but the smoke which approaches it will overcome it. We might say that, in some respects, this is a pathetic image in that it displays the futility of an impossible belief in meaning grounded in faith. Rather than transcendence, in this sense, the cross can come to signify a kind of pagan tokenism outstripped by the sophistication of the destruction signified by the explosion. Since the significance of the image is now neither true nor real, but rather an effect of the terms of the system that has produced both it, and our capacity to comprehend it, is open to question.

For Roland Barthes, the text understood as signifying in reaction to the sign, produces an understanding of the text which:

> practices the infinite deferment of the signified, is dilatory; its field is that of the signifier and the signifier must not be conceived of as 'the first stage of meaning', its material vestibule, but, in complete

> opposition to this, as its *deferred action*. Similarly, the *infinity* of the signifier refers not to some idea of the ineffable (the un-nameable signified) but to that of *playing*; the generation of the perpetual signifier (after the fashion of a perpetual calendar) in the field of the text (better, of which the text is the field) is realized not according to an organic progress of maturation or a hermeneutic course of deepening investigation, but, rather, according to a serial movement of disconnections, overlappings, variations.
>
> (Barthes 1990:158)

'Practices', 'action', 'playing', 'generation', 'hermeneutic', and finally 'disconnections, overlappings, variations'. All imply *operations*, suggesting that the text is, conceptually, a set of procedures, actions, processes, which are also interactive, multi-dimensional (hermeneutic – interpretive). 'Deferment', 'dilatory', 'infinity', 'perpetual', and finally 'serial movement', all imply time as a process, a movement which is both delayed ('dilatory') and perpetual or ongoing, potentially without end. 'Field' and 'vestibule' seem to connect operations and time with 'space' in which meanings can be said not to be fixed, but rather to reside, temporarily, on their way to somewhere else.

To unpick that process is no longer to reveal the veracity of a text, but rather to **trace** the impossibility of the logic by which its meaning may be fixed on the way to somewhere else. As an analysis of the supposed manifestation of the event '9/11' in representations of it, as a retrospective justification of the subsequent 'war on terror' which is aimed primarily at the Islamic world, this is compelling.

Writing as iterability

There have been a number of critiques of what might be termed the Saussurean paradigm of signification since it first appeared in 1916, but not all are necessarily well founded in any detailed reading of the text of *Course in General Linguistics*. While this makes the concepts of textuality and signification an *issue* in cultural criticism, it is important also to be aware of the terms by which any critique might be made.

One theorist who has thoroughly engaged with the detail of the *Course in General Linguistics*, while maintaining its significance throughout the twentieth century, is the French philosopher Jacques Derrida (1930–2004). Derrida's critique of Saussure's analysis is that it privileges speech over writing, and thus maintains a counter-productive reliance on the western metaphysical notion of **presence**. Speech, Derrida argues, is generally thought of as belonging more intimately and immediately to the *subject* that speaks. That is, speech is thought of in an inherent relation to experience, whereby it acts as a direct expression of it. This has a reciprocal effect in that it confirms both the subject and the experience enacted in speech as though each were manifest in and by the other. The operation of this privilege is apparent, for example, in the notions of the unquestioned veracity of 'testimony' over written accounts of events, since the act of writing is understood to place the event described at one remove from the immanence of speech. Consider the endless transmission of the mobile phone messages of the people caught up in the hijacking of the planes on September 11, or the eyewitness accounts of people in London who were there at the scenes of the bombings on 7 July. These were always more powerful than anything written about the same experience, both in the sense that they were privileged as such, but also that they were consumed as such. This matters to Derrida, since it reinforces a logic of presence through which, he argues, the whole of the metaphysics of the West is founded. Here, metaphysics signifies the system of structures which give rise to thought as conceptual possibilities of that system. In other words, it marks the terms and conditions of thought, as well as the particular understanding to which those conditions give rise, within the space and cultural traditions of what is currently designated 'the West'.

Derrida's task is to show that this functioning, this process of generating meanings, is not natural but rather an effect of the structure of signification itself which we might call writing. Without metaphysics of some sort, without the rules by which meaning can be generated, we would, quite literally, be unable to think. But this does not make the terms of that thinking inevitable. That speech is privileged over writing in **Western metaphysics** is a result of the dependence of that system on a notion of presence.

For Derrida, then, the privilege of speech is the privilege of an immanentism, regardless of where that privilege might operate. If we are to move beyond a metaphysical notion of thought as immanent to speech, we must move the focus of our analysis of signification from speech to writing.

Writing, for Derrida, depends on iterability. In a reading of the work of the Austrian psychoanalyst Sigmund Freud (1856–1939), in the essay, 'Freud and the Scene of Writing' (2004a), Derrida remarks that Freud's conceptualization of the psyche is produced through a notion of the text. 'What,' he asks, 'is a text, and what must the psyche be if it can be represented by a text?' (Derrida 2004a: 250). Moving within the text of Freud, Derrida's analysis reveals a fresh set of conceptual possibilities. The psyche for Freud, Derrida's reading suggests, is a kind of writing, which Freud himself had long been concerned to conceptualize in terms that might allow for thought to be reproduced 'mechanically'.[6] Here, the writing pad is a device for writing which involves placing a piece of paper, or something like paper, over a tablet of wax which, once written on with a blunt instrument, will make marks that can be read, but which can also be immediately erased by lifting the 'paper' from the wax and starting again. Experimenting with this metaphor of the writing pad, Derrida explores the difference that thinking of thought as writing might make.

While the 'writer', having made the marks on the pad which are then erased, may start again, Freud observes that the trace of the prior writing will always appear within the writing which follows. That is, there will still be a discernible residue in the wax of what has gone before. Seizing on this as both a way into Freud's notion of the psyche and as a demonstration of writing as a movement in time indelibly impressed by the trace of everything that has gone before it as writing, Derrida suggests that: 'There is no present text in general, there is not even a past present text, a text which is past as having been present. The text is not conceivable in an originary or modified form of presence' (2004a: 211). That the text is not conceivable in any originary or modified form of presence means that the text is never integrally present to itself and that, as such, it is never grounded by recourse to something outside of the system of writing which constitutes it, and which in turn can be said to be present.

This goes some way to accounting for Derrida's assertion elsewhere that 'There is nothing outside of the text' (1976: 158) which was later reworked as 'there is nothing outside of the context' (1988: 136).[7] That there is nothing outside of the text, foregrounds what was latent in Saussure, that there is nothing outside of the sign. That there is nothing outside of the context foregrounds the impossibility of either an inside to the text or of an outside, but rather that the text emerges as an ambivalence of the trace of both. That we think in terms of the inside/outside is nothing other than an effect of a metaphysics that privileges presence over absence rather than taking both as intrinsically relational conceptual terms.

That the work of the psyche is *like* that of writing in this sense, further displaces the notion of presence from the scene of writing, since one consequence of this is that the writer is also written. As such, constituted in part through the operation of the psyche as a layering of traces, 'we' are no longer conceivable as presence. Like the text, 'we' are opened to the continual displacement of the trace of what has been, as well as that of what is yet to come. Emerging from the often conflicting pressures of the relation between Freud's concepts of the conscious and unconscious, the subject is not only never fully present to itself, but also always in process, subject to the play of the trace, even in the very act of thinking of itself as such.

One consequence of this is that it can radically re-describe what we may think of as textual 'evidence'. It unsettles easy notions of history and, perhaps most especially, what we think of as *personal* history. And it particularly calls to account any apparently obvious function of memory within such textual evidence. Within this framework, something like 'history' can never serve as anything like the capture of the real, or even a moment within it, since it is always already a layering of traces and, as such, emerges as an effect of, and in turn a relation to, those traces. The photographs of people desperately running from the plumes of smoke which threaten to engulf them, by which '9/11' has come to be signified, can never be free from either the trace of inscriptions which have preceded them as text, or from the retrospectively imposed trace of those that follow. At the same time, the 'trauma', which those photographs are said to depict, becomes intelligible as such only by the act of writing the event which is itself also a form of textuality as an effect of the play of the trace. It makes sense as trauma, not because it either *is* or *is not* trauma in itself, but rather because it gets produced as trauma in reference to the particularities of its appearance as such.

This is not to say that trauma does or does not exist, but rather that what counts as trauma, in any culture at any given moment in time, radically depends on the traces of memory (themselves 'written') which serve to write trauma as such. In the case of the photographs of '9/11', these traces produce the effect of the memory of trauma from all other instances made intelligible as trauma. We might then say that without all of the reiterated images of spectacular explosions, signifying terror, trauma and the overcoming of evil forces which the dream-world of Hollywood has already written on us, such images as those of '9/11' would not be as readily intelligible to us in the ways they seem to be. But these images also depend, it can be argued, on a whole set of supposedly more real 'documentary' images which have also acquired something of an iconic status. These include, but are not exhausted by, images from the Europe of the Second World War, from Palestine and Belfast, the whole weight of 'Holocaust representation', and the nuclear devastation wreaked on Hiroshima in 1945.[8]

What becomes interesting in the process of signification which such photography enacts is that readings of them may include both the foregrounding and the disavowal of those traces. The resonance of the image of the little girl running from the mushroom cloud of atomic smoke in Hiroshima, for example, helps to signify trauma in the images of '9/11', but it must also be disavowed if we are to continue to think of '9/11' as the dehistoricized, de-contextualized, event of pure **humanistic** trauma, it has become. It must especially be disavowed if we are to think of '9/11' as a senseless act on an innocent world power.

History, in the sense of a record, then, does not exist in any pure or original moment of presence. It never did and it never will. That does not mean that we don't have a writing of history, just that we can no longer conceive of it as the mark either of a presence or of an absence. History, in these terms, is the structural repeatability of writing as a movement through time conceived not as a linear sequence, but rather as an ongoing process radically dependent on what has been written before as well as what will be written next. To borrow from the Derrida quoted earlier, there is no context to the text of history in this sense, just as there is no text of history to the context. Rather the conception of both is disrupted in such a way that the context is as textual as the text is contextual, even in the very moment of its inscription. Just like the writing pad, memory is nothing other than the trace of all writings which, while constituting it, also remain within it to shape what it is possible to signify.

This is possible for Derrida, since signification entails a structure of repeatability: 'a writing that is not structurally readable – iterable – beyond the death of the addressee would not be writing' (1988: 7). If writing must be iterable beyond the death of both the writer and the reader to whom it may be addressed, then writing must have its own *structural* logic independent of either intention or interpretation. This is clearly the case. I can email a friend before being killed by lightning, but that email is still readable by the friend after the event of my death. In the same way, it is still readable by anyone other than the friend, and this could include an entirely unrelated person, albeit differently and in ways unanticipatable in the moment of the writing. If this is the case, however, suggests that writing, the iterability of writing in order to *be* writing, refers only to its own structural logic of repeatability. In this sense, the text is not presence because presence itself is textual.

The psyche as textual in the sense of writing as Derrida conceives of it, also lends the concepts of textuality and signification a further significance in thinking 'the subject' as a subject of, and subject to, the movement of signification which Saussure first sought to analyse. That we might understand the subject *as text*, is a major issue for cultural criticism, since it displaces subjectivity from the grounds of presence, and thus opens it both to contingency, and to an absolute lack of veracity.

The subject as text

For Freud, human consciousness, as the consciousness of self conscious of itself as such, was always illusory. Since becoming conscious in this sense emerges only from the system of language (as cultural value) by which the very possibility of consciousness is already set out, consciousness is, by definition, the property of culture. While we enter the world as an unstructured animalistic being, we move reasonably rapidly from that state into a world of meaning which is the culture we inhabit. We do this, according to Freud, in a process of acquiring meaning which also entails the repression of socially unacceptable forces of the raw animal state. In the force of repression, the psyche of the signifying human is radically split between the conscious – obedient to the laws of signification – and the unconscious – which is not.

While this splitting of the psyche allows for the formation of a sense of self with a place in the world of meaning upon which we all depend, it also produces that sense as radically divided to itself. Understood in terms of the mystic writing pad, the psyche emerges from the erasures and traces which writing the psyche necessarily entails. And, as erasures are also always traces, they are, paradoxically, always present, even in their absence. In writing we can cross out the sign we wish to disavow – '~~me~~' – but the sign continues to operate in the spectre of its erasure. In my consciousness of myself, my being in the world as an effect of that consciousness can be erased, but I can never be sure that it is not still at work wherever that consciousness operates.

For Freud, the constitution of the psyche in these terms disrupts any notion of pure presence upon which it seems to depend. If the conscious emerges as an effect of the split from that which is signified in the concept of the unconscious, then it is always also an effect of the trace of the other within it.[9] It emerges, presents itself in the first place, as present only by virtue of a radical absence which it masks. It is not that the idea of self which emerges as a subject of meaning is *not* located metaphysically in presence, but rather that it is neither located in presence nor absence. Neither presence nor **absence**, the signifying human emerges as an effect of the unsteady relation between the two.

As a result, the subject is textual in the sense that it is an effect of the play of the trace, but also in that what it is, what it constitutes itself as, is not present to itself as such. The self which presents itself, does so only provisionally and incompletely. It is also further opened to interpretation, not least the interpretation of the symptoms it will display of something other than what it might believe itself to be. That I might think of myself as not racist, for example, does not mean that I am not. Indeed, it could be argued that I'd be the last to know, especially if my **ego** (my sense of myself) depends on an illusion that I am somehow constituted outside of the defiles of signification. In this example, my very sense of myself can be at stake in the accusation, and it is thus highly charged.

Interestingly, racism in this example also arises as an effect of the play of signification, and as such gets conceived of as a signifying operation, regardless of the apparent will or intent of the subject which signifies.

For the Martinican cultural critic and psychoanalyst Frantz Fanon (1925–61), this account of racism as signification also has parallels with the description he offers of how racism has operated in relation to his own self-perception. Writing in 'The Fact of Blackness', Fanon asserts that the 'fact' of 'blackness' is not in any sense a fact at all, but rather emerges as an effect of a contextual circulation and signification of 'blackness' which depends for its effect on the trace of all other significations now written as 'facts' which have gone before it. For Fanon, racism is entailed in the hostile gaze of an other which is able to read the embodiment of the black man as signifying a particular set of cultural values we might now call stereotypes.[10] Interestingly, these are, for Fanon, not simply located in the time of the moment of the racist glance in its now, but are rather construed in the layering effect of other referents themselves not referential (in the sense of being either real or true) but rather wholly contextual in the sense that Derrida has explored. Fanon writes of the moment of racist recognition/misrecognition:

> I was responsible at the same time for my body, for my race, for my ancestors. I subjected myself to an objective examination, I discovered my blackness, my ethnic characteristics; and I was battered down by tom-toms, cannibalism, intellectual deficiency, fetishism, racial defects, slave-ships, and above all else, above all: 'Sho' good eatin'.
>
> (Fanon 1991:112)

Fanon may conceive of himself as a human individual like anyone else at work within the world, but he comes to signify an object in the circulation of signs that generates the culture of Paris in the 1940s and 1950s. This circulation of signs is both historical and contemporary, a layered effect which is always already at work within the sign that the blackness of his skin comes to represent. This is not a fact, though it may appear to operate as though it is. It is neither real, nor true, but rather an effect of the iterability and indelibility of writing that produces cultural meaning.

Constituted as textual, subjectivity – consciousness of self in terms of the concept 'self' provided by language – becomes both an effect and an operation of signification. In some senses, this means that as signifying animals we are never in control. We can never say what we mean, or mean what we say, despite the necessary illusion that we can and do. As an issue, this will be developed more fully in the following chapters on aesthetics, ethics and the real.

However, before moving on, there is one more issue raised by the conceptualization of the subject as text which it is useful to briefly explore here. If subjects as text are open to rereading as signifying processes, then they are also open to the play of signification as an indirect effect. That is, they are open to, and in turn serve to refocus, a particular operation of signification which can no longer be overlooked: that of dissemblance. While we tend to think of signification in terms, such as 'literal' and 'metaphoric', there is a certain sense in which, given all of the above, signification is only ever metaphorical. Signification, in other words, never signifies directly, but always stands indirectly for something else through the processes of difference and association.

This is what makes it possible to read 'symptomatically' – to read, that is, for the symptoms that betray a meaning or set of meanings other than those overtly offered. This could be the symptoms of the human – the twitch in my left eye which manifests itself organically may well be read, in some instances, as a symptom of something other than the organic, perhaps psychic anxiety. This could be the human in speech or writing – where my constant reiteration, for example, of 'to be perfectly honest' might be read as a symptom either of an idea that I'm not being honest, even to myself, or of an anxiety that my listener/reader is not convinced. But, it could just as easily be a text in the more conventional sense of a photograph, poem or play. In this sense, the visual insistence on the focus of the cross in the photograph of '9/11' could be read not just as evidence of a dominant idea about Christianity and Islam, but also as an anxiety of something which the image continues to signify despite disavowing.

The issue of textuality and signification

Theories of textuality and signification clearly afford cultural criticism a set of frameworks for thinking about the objects of culture, our approach to those objects, and the ways in which meaning is made to circulate in a given culture via its objects. They also open up a space within which cultural criticism might act as a form of dissent, resisting the obvious or dominant meanings in circulation at any given time as common sense.

The issue for cultural criticism of thinking in terms of textuality and signification is also clear. If cultural criticism is to be more than a simple reiteration of cultural value in the appreciation of objects, whether positively or negatively, then it must begin to question the status of those objects as well as the ways in which they come to be constituted as such. In this sense, theories which address meaning in the very terms of its constitution, operation and effects, provide the possibility of engaging with the logic of those terms in order to resist and unsettle them. To work to show how particular meanings are produced as neither innate nor immovable is not simply to dismiss meaning as ideology – either to be agreed with as 'right', or to be dismissed as wrong. It is, rather, to work to show the terms by which any constitution of meaning is simultaneously possible and impossible, both transient and contingent, and in so doing to encourage a relation to culture which is relentlessly interrogative.

The value of unrelenting interrogation is the value of resistance which is not fully or finally determined, but which may remain open to the possibilities of future recirculations in ways it cannot imagine since they do not already fall, predictably, within its terms.

As the subject of a particular set of knowledges at this particular moment in time, for example, I am compelled to advocate a particular meaning for the process of signification through which the sign 'freedom' operates which insists on both its historical contingency and its differential global application. I might, of course, also be compelled by the **desire** of my ego to constitute itself through a quasi-liberal association, and be entirely unaware of that desire. Nothing, in either case, which has been argued in this chapter prevents me from doing this. What it does prevent me from doing, however, is claiming on behalf of that insistence, something which is free of value.

In insisting on the insistence, I am inevitably also foregrounding the cultural significance of the insistence. I am, in other words, foregrounding my arresting of the play of meaning in a particular way, on behalf of something other than itself, at a particular moment in time. This might be an equally arbitrary and imaginary notion of 'the people' – of Africa, say, or Iraq – and it may, as my use of inverted commas is intended to mark, have nothing whatever to do with any reality of the people of Africa or Iraq, as an intelligible entity within my discourse. Nonetheless, it works, in the sense that it produces an effect. It is possible, within the frameworks for thinking of textuality and signification explored here, to show that that effect comes about from the act of arresting the play of arbitrary relations within the metaphysics I inhabit, with the purpose of signifying something that may be contrary to more dominant versions of 'freedom' already in play. However, while signifying something, my insistence also draws attention to the function and effect of a particular use of the sign 'freedom'. It demonstrates the lack of coherence, the arbitrariness, by which it is constituted and through which it comes to signify. My insistence, then, is also contestatory in that it both draws attention to the inadequacies of the taken-for-granted signification, and at the same time suggests alternative possibilities which, based on a different set of values, may generate a very different signification.

However, there is still nothing necessarily fixed by the insistence thus made. It could be understood, even in the moment of its articulation, as temporary, open to change in different, as yet unanticipated, ways. I might in the future, wish to contest the value of the concept of 'freedom' itself, not just as relational but also as a concept valued in a particular way. What's so great about 'freedom' after all? What does it mean, on what might the conditions of its meaning be said to depend? What's at stake in the very concept of 'freedom' and what it might be said to imply for the condition of being human in the world of today? I don't currently believe, for example, that 'freedom' to kill people who disagree with me is inevitably a good thing. I might change my mind in a future I can't yet anticipate, but for now I'd be inclined to say that 'freedom' itself might just be an overvalued and mistaken category of thought in this respect.

That I can say any or all of this depends quite fundamentally on a conceptualization of signification as open, temporal, endlessly open to change, constituted textually, yet always in excess of that – *always*, as Barthes put it, 'paradoxical' (1990: 158).

One aspect of this discussion of theories of textuality and signification which has not been foregrounded is that of pleasure. That is, of the pleasure that may be entailed both in the play of signifying practices which textuality can afford, and in the encounter between the subject of culture and its objects. This encounter, the notions of pleasure, transformation and affirmations of 'self' made possible in the relation between subject and object in that encounter, are more precisely the subjects of exploration within the domain of aesthetics. The following chapter extends the notions of textuality and signification explored here, to examine more closely a further set of critical thinking signified by the term aesthetics. While some of these theories developed specifically to deal with 'art', they can nonetheless be expanded beyond that term, to consider the relation of the human to the world of its objects as it is constituted by culture more generally.

2 Aesthetics

- Why aesthetics?
- The sublime
- Estrangement
- The issue of aesthetics

Why aesthetics?

> Characters can bring about in one act what we in music cannot dream of – that people practice madly for ten years, completely fanatically for a concert, and then die. That is the greatest work of art for the whole cosmos.
>
> (Stockhausen 2001)

That the German composer Karlheinz Stockhausen (1928–) could remark of '9/11' that it was the 'greatest work of art for the whole cosmos' caused outrage around the world. Most obviously, his remarks were considered scandalous because they seemed to trivialize the suffering and shock that the events described as '9/11' have come to signify. It was not deemed appropriate, in the face of the scale of the event, to speak of it as a work of art. However, in another less obvious sense, his remarks were also considered scandalous since they seemed to have brought the concept of Art (with a capital 'A') into disrepute. Art, thought of as a set of high cultural texts, was displaced in this pronouncement onto the terrain of the vulgar, and this had to be recuperated.

What both Stockhausen's comments and the responses to them demonstrate, however, is a common concern with what art is, what art can do and what effects it may be said to generate. In both cases, art is presumed to be something in its own right, to perform something, and, as a consequence, to have effects which matter. That we can fight over what the terms of those presumptions should be does not detract from the commonality of those presumptions in the first place.

The presumptions that we make about art, or indeed the relation that we, as humans, have to the objects of the culture which surround us, have long been the subject of a particular branch of philosophical inquiry designated 'Aesthetics'. While developing from philosophy, however, 'aesthetics' has impacted on a number of academic fields which share concerns about what cultural objects are and how they might be thought to function. Fields, such as Fine Art and Art History, are obvious sites where theories of something like aesthetics can be found to be at work in constituting the field as a field of inquiry. English, perhaps, with its roots in the study of 'the great English classics' might also be said to have mobilized theories of aesthetics, if not overtly, then at least implicitly. Moving away from a notion of 'Art' as the representation merely of 'the beautiful', fields, such as those of Sociology and Anthropology, have asked what consumer objects and reified tokens may mean to the people for whom they circulate in particular social formations. All, in varying ways, involve assumptions and judgements which can be said to derive, in some way or another, from the study of aesthetics as a discrete activity.

For Karlheinz Stockhausen, art can be music and theatre as live and spontaneous, and it can be pleasurable and unpleasurable. It can confirm and it can unsettle. It can shock, alienate and distress. But it is art because it is in address to someone (singular or collective) and it produces effects which transform those who are addressed by it. In this, he is not too far removed from what philosophers and art practitioners have claimed about art from, at least, the time of the European Enlightenment and the Romantic movement which followed.

This chapter examines the developments of aesthetics and explores the issues at stake in different conceptualizations of what aesthetics is and what it does. From notions of 'art for art's sake', first explored by Immanuel Kant (1724–1804) in terms of 'things-in-themselves', through the dissonance of art as transformative catalyst, to more contemporary notions of representation as a 'thing-in-itself' in the idea of simulation, the analysis retains a focus on what might be called subject–object relations.[1] While a great deal of philosophy of aesthetics is broadly a philosophy of mind concerned with the status of philosophy as a system in its own right, this chapter will be concerned primarily with the possibilities of such philosophies for theorizing what counts as 'aesthetic' in culture and why. In doing this, the chapter sometimes takes art with a capital 'A' as its quarry, and sometimes the more mundane forms of cultural text considered vulgar by comparison. By treating both as objects through which cultures and subjects define themselves, the chapter also begins to establish a case for the role of aesthetics in cultural criticism which may not exactly have been anticipated by the work of the Romantic philosophers on which, among others, it draws.

The sublime

As a concept, the sublime emerges in its difference to the beautiful, yet both are held in a relation to something understood as experience, more particularly, aesthetic experience. Here, the beautiful comes to signify experience as pleasure which restores and confirms, while the sublime signifies pleasure as overwhelming, awesome in its power, and hence a thrilling entanglement of excitement and fear. It is in excess of the beautiful since the joy that it signifies can be ecstatic.

For the German philosopher Immanuel Kant, both the beautiful and the sublime involve a relationship between experience, understood as the internal effect felt by an encounter, and objects, understood as 'things in the world' which are encountered.[2] While Kant's theses on aesthetics centralize experience, they also explore the possibilities of it as a category which is not entirely integral to itself. Understood as a relation, experience becomes both confirming of the individual, present prior to the experience, and in some respects constitutive of it as an effect of a movement between the two terms of the relation within which it operates.

For Kant, aesthetics was a means of restoring the status of metaphysics which had fallen into disrepute in philosophy through the eighteenth century since it did not seem to be possible to grasp it and so to pronounce definitively upon it. What Kant sought to do, then, was to theorize afresh how we come, as humans, to 'know'. Underlying this project from the start was a shattering discovery, later accepted as fact, by a Polish astronomer in 1543. Using the mathematical theories of Pythagoras, Nicolaus Copernicus challenged the very basis of thinking in his time by proving that the earth was spherical and that it moved around the sun. On the basis of his account, the world, and so 'man', could no longer be thought of as the centre of the universe.[3] By displacing the centre from the earth to the sun, Copernicus also displaced the idea of man as the place from which all else stems. For Kant, this influenced what he theorized as perception. If man could no longer be thought of as determining the universe, then the universe, if not determining of man, must at least be held in a relationship to man which in some ways shaped the ways in which he was able to think. For Kant, the question became one of the relation between external objects and internal processes of perceiving those objects as mutually dependent relations: 'We must, therefore, make trial whether we may have more success in the tasks of metaphysics, if we suppose that objects must conform to knowledge' (1990: xvi). If Copernicus could prove that the universe does not exist for us as a thing in itself, but rather as an effect of what our systems of knowledge make possible to us, then perception is more than simply a way of looking at things. Perception, in other words, is not independent of things, but rather works to structure the things which it appears merely to 'see'. In this sense, perception could have a structure of its own which had hitherto been overlooked. Thought of as both structured and structuring, perception thus becomes a force which contributes to the things it perceives in the very process of perceiving them, even and perhaps most especially when perceiving them as if they were things in their own right. This denaturalizes perception, and with it experience, since neither can be said to be exercised independently of mind.

For Kant, there are two modes for human knowledge which he offers as 'sensibility' and 'understanding': 'Through the former, objects are given to us; through the latter, they are thought' (1990: 66). While this retains something of the notion that the object is constituted somewhere in the relation between object and perception, it also points towards the possibility of an existence for objects which is not determined, even reciprocally, by perception. By dividing sensibility from understanding, Kant thus provides the beginnings of an analysis of objects which can move beyond the function of mind to that of sensation as something which cannot necessarily be grasped by mind, but which nonetheless remains a vital aspect of experience. This not only transforms what experience can be, thought as a relation to mind, but also suggests that there might be objects which exist *in themselves*, independently from mind but with an effect on the organic being of body. While it is possible for Kant to conceive of the potential for objects-in-themselves as fully present within themselves – they are not transformed by the idea of them – such objects can, in turn, force the transformation of the mind which encounters them, by exposing its limits. Bypassing the rational structures of thought, objects which are 'given to us' from a place beyond the terms within which we think, cause us to recognize the limits of mind and so, paradoxically, to begin to address them by recourse to something more enduring, and so more fundamental to our existence as we can continue to conceive of it. Such objects, for Kant, produce an effect he calls 'the Sublime'.

In Roland Emmerich's 1996 blockbuster film, *Independence Day*, as the 'alien' spacecraft moves slowly towards the White House in its final, seemingly inevitable, gesture of mastery over it, there's a brief pause in the frenetic action of the film as the camera focuses indulgently on the underside of the 'ship' as it engulfs the screen and so our field of vision. The image is at once 'awesome' since it is bigger than anything so far depicted, and 'awe-some' since the sheer magnitude of it seems to signify its potential to destroy the Earth and with it 'us'. For the characters within the world which the film depicts, what will be left if the aliens triumph, is unthinkable. This is both because it cannot be known – it comes from a place *literally* beyond the world that we know – but also because they are reluctant even to imagine it, since it threatens to entirely overwhelm them by erasing them from their own existence. For the audience, for the duration of the image, the auditorium is filled by the sheer magnitude and detail of the visual experience and the tumultuous resonance of the sound that accompanies it. It can be described, for both the characters and the audience who watch them, as an instant in which the 'mind' is 'blown', and experience succumbs to the visceral.[4]

This approaches what the sublime can signify for Kant. While the beautiful is experienced via thought, the sublime exceeds the beautiful by recourse to a conception of sense beyond thought. If the 'thing-in-itself' institutes the sublime as sensory experience, however, it is also still thought of in a *relation* to mind, since it is encountered by humans for whom the mind–body dualism remains relational. While the mind exercises no authority over the object in the concept of the sublime, the object as 'thing-in-itself' has the capacity to jolt the mind by demonstrating that there is *more* than mind. The sublime effect, then, is not entirely isolated from mind, since it serves in relation to mind as another way of knowing, the recognition of which has the capacity to expand the scope of mind to grasp something like the real of existence.

If the distinction between 'sensibility' and 'understanding' serves to point to something outside of, or beyond, rational metaphysics, however, it remains nonetheless fully within it. In the realms of the sensible, objects are given to us. We do not constitute those objects, since they are beyond any process of shaping that metaphysics might perform. But they are 'there', and in being there, they are 'there for us'. They have a function in pointing out the inadequacies of thinking as it determines the world in our perception of it, but they also ground that thinking in a further relation to 'something' which is indisputably 'out there'. Human existence then conforms to the idea of that something by not quite living up to the transcendent perfection, or wholeness, of it.

In Kant, the 'beyond-ness' of the sublime implies a greater power than man, defiled by reason, since it simply *is*. This can be the raw power of nature beyond the control of man's capacity to organize and so to structure it, but it can also be a transcendent figure like god, whose power is protected as such by residing beyond the comprehension of mortal logic.

That the aesthetic experience of the sublime is that which bypasses the incompleteness of reason, also makes the sublime for Kant a means for human 'improvement', however that may be defined. In this sense, the sublime is 'given to us' as a chance to glimpse the real of our world, and so act accordingly.[5] It is difficult here to escape the consequences of either the act of 'giving', or the concept of a real which is founded upon it. Like miracles, or seemingly senseless natural disasters, the sublime acts to jolt man towards a greater awareness of the power of the real in his ordinary, yet comfortable, world of experience. And, in this respect, while the sublime is often painful and incongruent, it is also morally enhancing.

Opposed to beauty, the sublime may be formless in that it will exceed what we think of as limits and structures. While beauty may produce a harmony between object and a subject who encounters it, the sublime will be dissonant, often enacting a kind of violence on the senses of recognition which the former assumes. But, that formlessness, that dissonance and almost violent force of disruption, will also excite and thrill, taking pleasure to the limits of its own seemly form, in order precisely to point to something beyond it. For Kant, the difficulty remains of putting such a force into words so that it can be comprehended without becoming something other than what it simply *is*. Perhaps for this reason, his own examples are largely drawn from forces of nature, such as the terror, yet strange beauty, of violent and unpredictable storms, and the strange mixture of allure and repulsion they hold for humans.

In this respect, the comparison drawn with the film of *Independence Day* is a vulgar one. Yet it can, perhaps because of its vulgarity, point out something of what might be at stake in the issue of transcendence upon which the sublime in Kant comes to depend. If the shot of the spacecraft inspires awe in the film, it is quickly recuperated and its capacity to overwhelm is itself overwhelmed by what turns out to be a greater power than any other – that of the American administration. God, it would seem, in the space of some 200 years, has been replaced by the transcendent will of a particular people. And, the glib images of the world raised as one in giving thanks to the USA for its deliverance of them from evil, seems only to underline this as the film draws to its close. However, what the film seems to share with the sublime in the moment of the time of that shot of the spacecraft, is a common sense that being human somehow irrevocably involves a disturbing relation to the sense of an 'other' which, while confirming it, also threatens to outdo it. The figure of the alien in *Independence Day*, then, is both monstrous and strangely alluring, in that the thrill of extinction to which it gestures allows both the ecstasy of the fantasy of disappearing at the limits of ourselves, *and* the pleasure of the mastery that overcomes it. This may not entirely have been the effect of the sublime anticipated by Kant, but the guarantee of self in the possibility of losing oneself can be similarly confirming.

In terms of aesthetics, something of Kant's concept of the sublime can be seen to persist in G.W.F. Hegel's *Introductory Lectures on Aesthetics* (first published in 1886) which, while theorizing the absolute ideal of mind, rely on a notion of art as a vehicle for human transformation.

Famously characterized as the philosopher of **dialectical materialism**, Hegel's account of mind is one in which it proceeds by contradiction towards an Ideal or Absolute. The movement of the dialectic here is one in which mind transcends what alienates it from itself through the process of encountering and ultimately resolving contradiction. For Hegel (1770–1831), this process involves the repetition of stages within which what he calls the 'Spirit' (*Geist* in German, which can also be translated as mind) reflects on the state of itself, but in doing so also transcends that state by responding to the inadequacies it reveals. Thus a new state is developed which can in turn be reflected on again, and so give rise to further development until an Ideal of perfection is realized. When that state is achieved, the process will be complete and a perfect state, no longer open to, or in need of, reflection is achieved.

This process has since been encapsulated in three terms which Hegel himself did not use, but which can be useful in grasping the schema of the dialectic at work in his thinking – thesis, antithesis, synthesis. In the first term, mind reflects on what it knows and finds that this is open to dispute by the second term; this prompts the resolution of the dispute in the synthesis produced as the third term. However, that third term then takes the place of the first as the subject of another reflection which can also be found wanting by the possibility of another version of the second term, so prompting the generation of another synthesis in a new third term. This is an ongoing process of gradual refinement.

While Hegel's process foregrounds the incompleteness of mind to itself, it also holds out the promise that through increasingly acute awareness of its own inadequacies, mind may eventually perfect itself. What is real here is still beyond mind in the first instance, as it was for Kant, but it can eventually be grasped by mind which, in a process of what Hegel called 'Entfremdung' (**estrangement**) from itself, may eventually return to itself in full awareness of existence stripped of mere illusion.

Again, objects understood as existing in a relation to man play a part in this process of thinking, or knowing, for Hegel as they did for Kant. This time, however, the inadequacies of mind to which they allude become the motivation for mind to perfect itself.

Art, in this sense, plays a role in the perfection of mind only if it has the power to shock and to alienate mind from its usual complacency. Here, objects cannot be the 'things-in-themselves' that Kant sought to realize, since they have no existence for Hegel which is truly independent of mind in the same way. In his *Introductory Lectures on Aesthetics*, Hegel comes to argue both that poetry is the highest form of art, in the sense of the role he ascribes for art, and that poetry must eventually concede to philosophy the task of moving the human mind to the point of an Ideal.

In the first place, poetry is the highest form of art since it is in poetry that Hegel finds 'the element . . . common to all forms of art' yet dictated by it – the 'imagination' to think beyond the confines of mere representation:

> Poetry is the universal art of the mind which has become free of its own nature, and which is not tied to its realization in external sensuous matter, but expatiates exclusively in the inner space and inner time of the ideas and feelings. Yet just in this its highest phase art ends by transcending itself, inasmuch as it abandons the medium of a harmonious embodiment of mind in sensuous form, and passes from the poetry of imagination into the prose of thought.
>
> (Hegel 1993: 96)

In the second place, poetry ends up transcending itself by abandoning the harmony of sensuous form in which something like beauty becomes a comfortable reassurance. For thought to continue its dissonant progress, poetry marks the exhaustion of art and its accession to critical thinking. Art is thus a stage in mind's perfection of itself, but not its completion.

For Kant, then, the sublime points the way to the essence of existence in something other than existence, outside of itself, which marks its limits; for Hegel, poetry prompts the dialectical process of refinement of mind by marking something beyond mind which, while alienating it from itself momentarily, can in the bigger picture be said to return it to itself in better shape than it was before. In each, art as object is differently constructed, yet in both it is held in a relation to something beyond itself which has the capacity to enhance the existence of man in his time spent on Earth.

Both Kant and Hegel were writing with concerns about the status of art in subject-object relations, which may seem remote to cultural criticism today. However, the work of both laid foundations for thinking about art, and about man's relation to the objects in the world, today. They certainly seem to haunt the assessment of '9/11' as art, with which this chapter began.

One 'postmodern' philosopher who draws on the work of the sublime begun by Kant, for example, is Jean-François Lyotard (1924–98).[6] Noted more for his account of the dissolution of the legitimating powers of grand narratives in what he termed 'the postmodern condition', Lyotard also produced a number of philosophical accounts of aesthetics, most notably in *Lessons on the Analytic of the Sublime* (1994) and *The Assassination of Experience by Painting – Monory* (1998).[7] For Lyotard, the condition of postmodernity signified by the collapse of the age-old legitimating narratives of God, science, even Marxism as guarantors of meaning, is not entirely dissociated from the question of 'the state of aesthetics' today.[8] With the decline of the grand narratives, and with them the last vestiges of belief in a 'something' located securely beyond the corruptions of 'worldly' comprehension they had served to signify, the very possibility of grounding meaning seems to have disappeared.

For Lyotard, this condition was not a reason for mourning as it was for Hegelian-Marxist critics, such as Fredric Jameson (1934 –).[9] Rather, the collapse of the power of these narratives was always already at work within them in their function of producing an illusion of meaning to mask its absence. In Lyotard's terms, the narratives of modernity collapsed by implosion, needing no help from any outside force, such as capitalism, or a rapidly growing technology of media culture. They collapsed as an effect of their own internal contradictions as signifying systems, finally exhausting their own capacity to 'pretend' to be meaningful. For Lyotard, the grand narratives were always only narratives, and as such were always already an impossible referent in the chain of signification they were supposed to arrest.[10]

Lyotard finds the condition of our contemporary paradoxically the same as that of any other moment of a contemporary. This time, however, it is a condition shorn of any illusion that there is something 'out there'. What Lyotard finds by way of his reports on both knowledge and aesthetics, then, is that the condition of postmodernity is the condition of an encounter with the real as a 'nothing', rather than a 'something', beyond comprehension.

In this sense, Lyotard's conceptual debt to both Kant and Hegel is clear in different ways. Kant was wrong about the sublime as an encounter with the 'thing-in-itself' beyond the comprehension of mind; and Hegel, while right about mind, was nonetheless wrong about its capacity to perfect itself in a dialectical process producing an awareness as, finally, fully present to itself. Both were right, it would seem, in conceiving of a beyond to knowledge, but they were wrong to conceptualize that beyond as a something rather than a nothing. As Lyotard examines the beyond of metaphysics, what he finds there is a kind of abyss.[11] In that finding, however, he maintains the concept of a 'beyond' which was so crucial to the theories he explicitly contests.

In his return to Kant, Lyotard privileges the 'indeterminate' aspects of the sublime as a disharmonious 'pleasure mixed with pain, a pleasure that comes from pain', creating within the subject that encounters it 'a kind of cleavage ... between what can be conceived and what can be imagined or presented' (1993: 98). While he draws explicitly on Kant, however, Lyotard also attempts to move beyond some of the implications inherent in Kant's conceptualization, in particular, the idealism latent in the idea of the sublime as a limitless capacity of mind as yet unrealized. What this implies for Lyotard is a conception of time as itself somehow outside of metaphysics rather than an effect of it. Time, in this sense, is one more transcendent in need of critique.

For Lyotard, time is not natural, as was assumed by Kant, nor is it progressive in the sense of the linear progression from past to present to future, implied by Hegel. For it to be either, time would have to stand outside of the structures for thinking time which produce it. While we tend to think of time as obvious, for Lyotard it is, like signification, an effect of difference, and as such, it is fully conceptual. Time is always, he argues, already beyond its sell-by date, since it never actually 'happens'. Each moment of 'now' is produced only in relation to other moments of 'now' in a series of 'nows' held, linguistically, by the absences of both the 'once now' of the past, and the 'yet to be now' of the future. The present-instant, present to itself in the moment of itself, is impossible since it 'tries to hold itself between the future and the past, and gets devoured by them' (1993: 90). Like the sign in the movement of the chain of signification, the present of the present-instant is determined by other present-instants which have preceded it and which also, therefore, expose the impossibility of its presence to itself. But it is also deferred by a relation to another 'now' which is always also 'yet to come'. Any 'present-instant', then, gets to be what it is only by virtue of a movement of difference which, while making it possible, simultaneously reveals its impossibility in the temporality that time itself necessarily entails. 'Now' is thus devoured by the very conditions which make it possible in the first place. What is revealed in this account of time is the absence, the radical lack of presence, of a core which the conceptual terrain of time continually strives to mask.

This bears directly on art and on the concept of the Kantian sublime in particular. Maintaining Kant's notion of the sublime as an indication of something beyond comprehension, Lyotard retains the sense of terror invoked there, while expunging from it the notion of presence involved in the 'thing-in-itself'. In place of the incomprehensible 'thing', Lyotard inscribes the 'no-thing' of an insurmountable lack:

> Terrors are linked to privation: a privation of light, terror of darkness; privation of others, terror of solitude; privation of language, terror of silence; privation of objects, terror of emptiness; privation of life, terror of death. What is terrifying is that *It happens that* does not happen, that it stops happening.
>
> (Lyotard 1993: 99)

Unlike the terror of the sublime, mitigated by Kant, in the pleasure of a kind of knowing that we are not all there is to the world, for Lyotard the terror invoked here is utterly unremitting. No longer grounded in a sense making referent outside of itself, a *something* in the beyond to which the sublime in Kant points, the terror invoked by Lyotard is the terror of the encounter with the abyss – there is nothing, limitless nothing, out 'there'.

Art can serve the purpose of masking this absence by ameliorating the terror it incites in creating an illusion, that it represents something and itself attests to the present-sense of meaning in its very existence as such. Avant-garde art, on the other hand, if it succeeds in jolting the viewer/reader out of the comfortable realms of the illusion, can work, for Lyotard, with a radical potential to disrupt and unsettle. In this sense, the avant-garde (literally, before its time) works not to reconcile sense with thought, but rather to reveal the impossibilities of presence at work in both. Its project is not simply to question human 'perception', but rather to question whether perception is anything other than an illusion covering its own impossibility. The question of the avant-garde, then, is not the question of what art is, or what it does, but rather the much more threatening question for Lyotard of, 'is it happening?' (1993: 103). Here, the relation between subject and object becomes one of analogy. If the object is not happening, then am I? The glimpse by the subject of its own disappearance in the operation of the sublime is here reworked in order to be unrecoverable, since there is nothing imagined to be up to the task.

What Lyotard writes about time in his account of aesthetics as the disappearance of appearance in this sense works equally well for him here in relation to the apparent 'matter' of sense as it does to mind.[12] The two are no longer separable, since they are always already not really there by virtue of the very relations which make it possible to 'experience' them in the first place.

Writing in 'After the sublime, the state of aesthetics', Lyotard argued that matter is a paradox, in that it is not 'finalized, not destined', but rather, like time, an effect of the difference that constitutes it:

> Nuance and timbre are scarcely perceptible differences between sounds or colours which are otherwise identical in terms of the determination of their physical parameters. This difference can be due, for example, to the way they are obtained: for example, the same note coming from a violin, a piano or a flute, the same colour in pastel, oil or watercolour. Nuance and timbre are what *differ* and *defer*, what makes the difference between the note on the piano and the same note on the flute, and thus what also defer the identification of that note.
>
> (Lyotard 1993: 141)

Stated like this, matter becomes, paradoxically, immaterial. It is, in time, never that which is either present or presentable. It is, rather, always yet to come.[13]

The avant-garde, for Lyotard, is art which does not conceal the immateriality of meaning, but rather incites and multiplies it. The sublime of the avant-garde is thus terrifying in its display of the impossible absence at the heart of what once seemed to be things, present to themselves in a present being which was not open to the vagaries of time.

Opened to the vagaries of time, on the other hand, the avant-garde provides a glimpse of a beyond to the illusion of experience, and of the being founded in that illusion, as nothing. But, is this really all there is? Lyotard, in his suggestion of a 'beyond' to metaphysics, seems to suggest that while time is conceptual, space is not. But, if it is possible to open experience to the contingency of time, then surely we can open experience still further to the vagaries of what we might call 'space'. If space is limitless, or infinite, then it too cannot be thought of as a 'thing-in-itself'.

If space cannot be thought of as a thing-in-itself, then there can be no sense to the concept of a beyond, which is delimited by it. Beyond, and nothing, thus come to be constituted in the same illusion of presence which Lyotard has decentralized for time. If we think of space as relational, as Lyotard asks us to with time, then the concepts of presence and absence disappear from the scene of space, and the notion of a 'beyond' comes to rest conceptually in a corresponding notion of a present – 'here' – upon which it can be said to depend for its own existence as such.

Art, thought of as providing a glimpse of the void of nothingness it masks, is still art which is thought to manifest a something, even if that something is nothing. While Lyotard's account of the sublime sets out to carve the radical possibility of its signifying nothing, it ends in implying the very presence it disavows in the form of the negative dialectic of a present-nothing. As the German cultural critic, Theodor Adorno, had argued in his own treatise on *Negative Dialectics* in 1966, nothing always manifests something, even if that something emerges from the dialectic of presence in negative terms. As Derrida also later pointed out, the negation of presence in the invocation of absence is itself inevitably caught in the metaphysics of presence since it retains the sense of presence in absence as not, temporally, present. That is, absence becomes a *form* of presence in that, in order to be absent in a present-moment, it must paradoxically be capable of being present in another time. In Derrida's account, a simple reversal of the terms of a differential relation by which meaning is generated does not critically engage the terms of that relation, it merely shifts them around and in so doing, maintains both them and the logic which sustains them.

There is something of this in Lyotard's aesthetics beyond Kant. The sublime as 'indeterminate', is indeed, the sublime as difference and deferral. But there is also a sense that there is something beyond this, something transcendent which, while it cannot be fully comprehended, is nonetheless indicated. In his conclusion to 'After the sublime, the state of aesthetics', Lyotard writes:

> From this point of view, theory, aesthetic theory, seems, will have seemed to be the attempt by which the mind tries to rid itself of words, of the matter that they are, and finally of matter itself. Happily, this attempt has no chance of success. One cannot get rid of the Thing. Always forgotten, it is unforgettable.
>
> (Lyotard 1993: 143)

For all of its linguistic diversions, this conclusion seems to posit a something, a **Thing**, which is beyond language. We cannot arrive at that Thing, since we'd have to be outside of representation, and that is literally unthinkable, but we can be stimulated to approach it, it is 'there'. It is 'there' perhaps as no more than a sense, in the presentation of the unpresentable. What the Thing is can be elusive in Lyotard, probably because it's more of an 'anti-thing' than a thing in itself. But, what does it imply, conceptually, if it pertains to the real? What does it imply about the real if it can be perceived, albeit fleetingly, by something thought of as 'sense'? While I have no desire to deny the real as such, the importance of the real as actually *present in* something beyond language and **symbolic** representation seems somewhat problematic. It seems to generate a certain idea of there being a Thing beyond signification which can be sensed and still hankered after nostalgically. At the very least, the Thing would have to be constitutive of all representation in its relation to the impossibility of the Thing. In which case, would it be a Thing at all?

That Lyotard capitalizes what he writes as the 'Thing' here points to a further set of concepts in critical and cultural theory which will be explored in Chapter 5 in relation to the real.

It may well be that the logic of the sublime itself, however we define it, retains the logic of the metaphysics it seeks to dispute. In this sense, neither the form nor the content of the sublime is inevitably radical. Nor, by implication, is the art of the avant-garde said to rise from its terms, and so to confirm them.

The poetry of dada may provide one example. In a poem credited to Tristan Tzara, dada defines itself ironically in its inability to be defined. In the movement of the time of the poem, dada emerges as that which resists definition:

> DADA is a virgin microbe
> DADA is against the high cost of living
> DADA
> Limited company for the exploitation of ideas
> DADA has 391 different attitudes and colours according to the sex of the president
> It changes – affirms – says the opposite at the same time – no importance –
> Shouts – goes fishing.
> Dada is the chameleon of rapid and self-interested change.
> Dada is against the future. Dada is dead. Dada is absurd. Long live Dada.
> Dada is not a literary school, howl
>
> (Tzara 1992)

But, in resisting definition, dada still *is*, since it manifests itself by what it is not. That's great fun to read and to think about because it foregrounds the paradox and plays with its own non-sense. But it's not necessarily terrifying or radical. Somehow, I am able to maintain a sense of myself in relation to it, even if that is a logical impossibility allegorized by the writing itself.

I'm afraid that the 'event' of '9/11' fares no better in this respect, although a number of cultural critics have suggested that it does.[14] Even in the depiction of the event as art in Stockhausen's account of it, there's little to really trouble the subject by way of an encounter with the impossibility of its own meaning, even in the ultimate act of self-annihilation which is said to have been performed there. While '9/11' may be the most widely consumed sign in Western culture at present, it is strangely devoid of the terror of an encounter with the nothingness of the real which, for Lyotard, the sublime is meant to be.

What *may* be more terrifying for a subject addressed by objects which surround them, on the other hand, might be found in a relation generated by that address which gives rise to indeterminate consequences. Where meaning can be determined and imposed, even retrospectively, the certainty of meaning can be maintained. Where meaning seems dislocated from itself, within itself proves more difficult to deal with. If it is more difficult to deal with, however, this does not necessarily mean that it is not in some way surmountable by the subject held in relation to it, but it does change the terms of the function of the object. In these terms, a more obvious, even vulgar, text which could never be thought of as avant-garde, might produce effects that are potentially more terrifying than any discussed so far. A populist film, such as *Scream*, for example, might be terrifying in a different sort of way. It can be terrifying *not* because it either confirms the harmony of the existence of the subject/viewer as either being present or absent to itself, but rather because of its foregrounding of a possibility that allows for *neither*. Alive and in control, I'm comfortable with. Dead and lacking control, I'll come to terms with, especially since it hasn't happened to *me* yet. Estranged *within* myself, radically at odds not with but rather within any notion of self founded in either presence or absence, is literally unthinkable.

This concept of estrangement within is not entirely unrelated to the issue of aesthetics, since it comes to unsettle the notion of the aesthetic relation and of experience itself, on which the concept of the sublime rests. Tracing its development in a different set of ideas, the *Entfremdung* which Hegel recuperates in his depiction of time as the progress towards the Ideal, can move through Nietzsche and Freud to a very different framework for analysis within which the condition of subjectivity as the neither/nor of matter and mind is called to account.

Estrangement

The German writer and philosopher Friedrich Nietzsche (1844–1900), really seemed to have laid his cards on the table, when he announced in 1887, that 'God is dead' (1974: 181). While this reference has entered popular discourse as something of a slogan, it's worth briefly locating what it signifies in relation to some aspects of Nietzsche's work which may help to reconfigure the issue of aesthetics for critical and cultural theory.

As a philosopher, Nietzsche has been remembered in some quarters as a 'perspectivist' whose work gives rise to an unbearable relativism. While there can be a certain sort of 'anything goes' to some of Nietzsche's particularly playful works, however, there is also a trenchant critical engagement with some of the key terms of philosophy at work there. Nietzsche was often scorned as a philosopher because of a concern with language which he placed on the agenda of philosophy as a 'proper' site of inquiry for it.[15] Nietzsche also critically engaged with the branch of philosophy known as idealism, of which Kant and Hegel were a part. What Nietzsche questioned there were the terms through which notions of 'truth', 'imagination', and the 'real' of the world came to be established.

For Nietzsche, the 'will to power' represents a basic drive in all forms of human being and in all forms of what counts as human achievement, including philosophy. Here, the 'will to power' is a kind of life force for Nietzsche, the drive that keeps the force of life alive. Concepts which ground that force, in truth, in the real, the imagination, and so on, are therefore, life-denying in Nietzsche's sense, since they represent attempts to organize that force in the service of reason. They are, Nietzsche asserts, an attempt by the weak (those whose life force is not sufficient to resist reason) to dominate the 'strong' and 'healthy' (those whose life force, by contrast, abounds). Such concepts are also, importantly for Nietzsche, *invested*. That is, far from being the abstract effect of pure reason by which they seem to announce themselves, concepts, such as 'truth', serve to hide the 'will to power' that motivates them. 'Truth', in Nietzsche's schema, then, becomes something which operates in the interests of asserting a particular set of values as the only possible values for humans to hold: 'Beyond all logic and its seeming sovereignty of movement, there also stand valuations or, more clearly, physiological demands for the preservation of a certain type of life' (Nietzsche 1990: 2–3). Here, truth stands in for value – something it also disavows – and works in the service of a particular 'type of life'. Bearing in mind Nietzsche's commitment to the concept of the ***Übermensch***, and of the 'will to power' manifest in 'truth' as the will of the weak to master the strong, the 'physiological demands' of the certain type of life asserted here provide no basis of succour for the weak as we may understand it more commonly today.[16]

In the sense that Nietzsche largely seems to provide, truth is displaced from the ground of a transcendental or universal meaning, onto a ground which is both relative and invested by power.[17] All truth, wherever it is asserted, becomes a perspective which stems from the 'will to power'. In these terms, truth is never life-affirming. In part, truth works to quell the life force that Nietzsche champions by imposing limits upon it. In his framework, thinking is inseparable from the structures of the metaphysics which produce it as possible in the first place. Here, thinking is inseparable from language for Nietzsche, since it is through language, he argues, that a culture comes to impose an artificial order on raw experience. Language, as Saussure was later to put it, performs the operation of cutting and structuring the 'vague and uncharted nebula' of the world before its appearance. What is truth, in this sense, Nietzsche asks but:

> A mobile army of metaphor, metonyms, and anthropomorphisms – in short, a sum of human relations, which have been enhanced, transposed, and embellished poetically and rhetorically, and which

> after long use seem firm, canonical, and obligatory to a people: truths are illusions about which one has forgotten that that is what they are.
>
> (Nietzsche 1954: 46–7)

That truths are illusions whose status we forget, suggests both that truth is paradoxically false, and at the same time that it serves illegitimately to guarantee only the values of those who mobilize it. Far from affirming any life force, truth becomes equated with the death of that force, as a form of unregistered murder.

Nietzsche's remark that 'God is dead', may be understood in terms of the relation of the sign, 'God', to the concept of truth, produced as it is only in language. If language is merely the structural division of raw experience, so as to organize it according to a set of dominant values, then any concept of truth so produced will be subject to the structures *of* language. This makes truth a vulnerable category. In order to protect this fundamental category, culture and in particular philosophy, grounds it in recourse to a further category supposedly untouched by the system. If language is open to the conditions of the system which produces it – metaphors, metonyms and anthropomorphisms – then its final validity can only be secured by a relation to something thought to be outside of the system that language is, which in this case, is God. God is, in this sense, *above* everything, at least in a certain metaphysics which operates in the interests of a certain set of values.

If God is dead, then there is no transcendental sign within which meaning may be understood simply to be true. God has ceased to work as transcendental in this sense, Nietzsche argues, in part because philosophy itself has killed God in its analysis of the function the sign is said to represent. Interestingly, the statement about the death of God is made in the course of a passage in *The Gay Science* headed 'The Madman' (1974: 181–2). Here the madman reports not on the death of God, but rather on the murder of God which he understands as the greatest achievement of one generation to bequeath to the next:

> The madman jumped into their midst and pierced them with his eyes. 'Whither is God?' he cried; 'I will tell you. *We have killed him* – you and I. All of us are his murderers ... What were we doing when we unchained this earth from its sun? Whither is it moving now? Whither are we moving? Away from all suns? Are we not plunging continually? Backward, sideward, forward, in all directions? Is there still any up or down? Are we not straying through an infinite nothing? Do we not feel the breath of empty space? ... Do we hear nothing as yet of the gravediggers who are burying God? Do we smell nothing as yet of the divine decomposition? Gods, too,

> decompose. God is dead. God remains dead. And we have killed him'.
>
> (Nietzsche 1974: 181)[18]

At the end of the madman's reported speech, it is told that he took his cry of the death of God to the churches, proclaiming, when asked what he was thinking of, 'What, after all are these churches now if they are not the tombs and sepulchers of God?' (1974: 182). Here, the churches seem to stand for philosophy, God for truth and the madman for Nietzsche upbraided by philosophy for his critique of it.

While Nietzsche never actually proclaimed the death of philosophy, as Hegel had done of art, philosophy's continual grounding of itself in the death of a concept it has itself killed, made philosophy for Nietzsche a less fertile terrain of inquiry. Any dividing line between the formal properties of art and philosophy is never clear in Nietzsche's work, but in one tome he turned explicitly to literature as a means of exploring what philosophy seemed, for him at least, to disavow. In *The Birth of Tragedy*, Nietzsche claims for art a special sort of metaphysical inquiry, based as it is not in truth but illusion. 'Art,' he writes, 'must insist on the purity of her domain . . . only as an esthetic phenomenon may existence and the world appear justified' (1995: 89).

For Nietzsche, tragedy, as form, revolves around a discordant relation between two forces which he terms, in reference to the Greek tradition on which he draws, 'Apollonian' and 'Dionysian':

> We shall do a great deal for the science of esthetics, once we perceive not merely by logical inference, but by the immediate certainty of intuition, that the continuous development of art is bound up with the *Apollonian* and *Dionysian* duality: just as procreation depends on the duality of the sexes, involving perpetual strife with only periodically intervening reconciliation.
>
> (Nietzsche 1995: 1)

Here, the duality which drives art is the duality of competing life forces which, as we have seen, is one foundational aspect of Nietzsche's philosophy of the state of life in the world. One might argue that while the difference of biological sex might be a raw material reality of life, the structure of gender imposed by culture institutes only on the value of that culture in nature. The sexism thus, latent in Nietzsche's remarks may be somewhat ameliorated. Given Nietzsche's remarks elsewhere on women and men, however, this is probably not sustainable.[19] Nonetheless, the distinction drawn here might remain in any case, since it is a distinction drawn between what we might call the 'drives' of human existence and the 'desires' of that existence inculcated in it by culture's displacement of them.

Both the Apollonian and the Dionysian life forces exist for Nietzsche in an inextricable relation. While in theatre and music you cannot have one without the other, what theatre and music become as a result, thereby foregrounds the genesis for their existence and for human existence in the principle of dissonance. Further, dissonance is not simply the encounter between two contradictory forces, but rather the trace of the other *within* each. It is not just that the Apollonian represents harmony and the Dionysian chaos, but rather that being is expressed in the inevitable conjunction of the two. Art, rather than philosophy, may play with the possibilities of this conjunction in ways which display their simultaneity, and which for philosophy would be unbearable within it. Art is able to do this since it foregrounds illusion: 'through which we are to be saved from an immediate oneness with the Dionysian music, while our musical excitement is able to discharge itself on an Apollonian domain and in an interposed visible middle world' (1995: 88).

In this way, 'the science of aesthetics' which Nietzsche seeks to contribute to, in turn also has a contribution to make to metaphysics, or perhaps more specifically to ontology, as it addresses the question of human existence:

> Music and tragic myth are equally the expression of the Dionysian capacity of a people, and are inseparable from each other. Both originate in a sphere of art lying beneath and beyond the Apollonian; both transfigure a region in whose joyous harmony all dissonance, like the terrible picture of the world, dies charmingly away ...
>
> At the same time, just as much of this basis of all existence – the Dionysian substratum of the world – is allowed to enter into the consciousness of human beings, as can be surmounted again by Apollonian transfiguring power, so that these two art-impulses are compelled to develop their powers in strict mutual proportion, according to the law of eternal justice.
>
> (Nietzsche 1995: 91)

Art, then, has a dual function in what we might now call Nietzsche's aesthetics. On the one hand, it is motivated, driven, by the raw and chaotic Dionysian life-force of the 'substratum of the world'. On the other, it is at the same time only possible as an expression of such by virtue of its relation of tension to the Apollonian force of structure. As such, art is both a space within which an eternal struggle is displayed, and from which a sense of that struggle may be encountered safely in the terms of the illusion that is art.

Something of Nietzsche's philosophical deconstruction of truth, and of his depiction of the human condition in terms of an irrevocable struggle *within* existence, is echoed in the later work of the Austrian psychoanalyst

Sigmund Freud. Both the theory of the human psyche that emanates from Freud, and subsequent theories of the function and effect of art in relation to that theory, revolve around the concept of a human being as radically divided within itself. If there is anything of a beyond to metaphysics in Freud, it is located firmly within metaphysics and, therefore, within the human which arises as a subject of that metaphysics.

The split in human mind instituted by its move from the raw existence of infant animalism to the structuring of that existence in the symbolic systems of culture, has briefly been encountered already in the preceding chapter on textuality and signification. However, the consequences of that split – between conscious and unconscious – can be elaborated here as the force which keeps the human in culture perpetually in a process of becoming that which it is impossible for it to master. Here the trace of the unconscious within the conscious it helps to found in the process of repression, works continually to unsettle the fullness of presence of the conscious to itself that the foundation of the ego (as sense of self) of the subject demands.

This radical incompleteness in the subject – the division within it which founds it – shifts the terms of aesthetics, especially as it conceptualizes the subject–object relation. If the subject is always already divided within itself, estranged in Hegel's sense, then not only is perception an effect of that estrangement, but the relation to objects in the world of culture is inevitably also constructed in its terms. Objects are no longer 'things-in-themselves', or at least not for us, but become the means by which we appear to discover ourselves in them. What perception always already entails in this model of the estranged subject in culture is the struggle of the ego to maintain itself even in the possibility of its own undoing.

If we think, not of art, but of consumer goods as objects in this sense, then something of the implication of Freud's thesis may become clear. In these terms, an object, such as a Ferrari Enzo, may be invested by its owner with something of an ideal version of their ego projected onto it. The car can be a thing of beauty in the imagination, but it comes to be so in part because of a particular perception of it as such which will necessarily entail the finding of an imagined ego within it. That has nothing necessarily to do with the Ferrari as a 'thing-in-itself'. If the Ferrari was not there, the ego could transfer the function of it onto another object in order that the object thus found, could be invested by the same ideal and so attempt the same amelioration of the estrangement of the ego from itself.

This is not simply a matter of perception *making* the object, as it is in Kant, although it can certainly include that. Perception in Freud's sense is itself not entirely a thing in itself either, since even the means by which it is constituted in the subject is neither present to itself as such nor complete. That we 'feel' that it is so is merely the work of the ego. In this sense, even the feeling apparently evoked by the object – of mystery, awe, something beyond itself to which it points – will depend on what does or does not threaten the ability of the ego to do its own impossible work.

The work of the ego is impossible in the sense that its achievement in the subject – a sense of self as present to itself – is temporal. The Ferrari Enzo as object may help to achieve that, and the ego of subject constituted in its relation to it may well be filled with a sense of contentment, that all is well with themselves and with the world, as they polish it in their driveways. It will only be a matter of time, however, before the sense of satisfaction the ego finds there will be exhausted in it and the search begins again to find the one magic object to end all objects. That feeling, paradoxically, comes not from outside the subject but from within it, not as an effect of the object in itself but as an effect of the estrangement that founds the possibility of the subject in the first place. What one ego finds beautiful and comforting, may prove deeply unnerving to another since it works, unbeknown to the subject founded in that ego, as a reminder of all that threatens its own undoing.

While there are many analyses in Freud's work of the status of objects in relation to the subjects who consume them, when it comes to art, there are two major conceptual frameworks for thinking about what we may term the aesthetic: the dream-work and the uncanny.

Dreams are not, for Freud, as it is sometimes assumed, direct manifestations of the unconscious. This is important to grasp in terms of the process of signifying what dreams represent for Freud. The unconscious is, semantically and conceptually, precisely *un*-conscious. The subject can never be conscious of the unconscious, except in the terms of the conscious where the unconscious, by definition, cannot be itself. That we might as subjects feel ourselves to be aware of something other than ourselves is, for Freud, an effect of the play of the trace of that otherness, within the self. As such, while effects of the trace may be 'felt', they cannot be comprehended except in the metaphysics of consciousness. In this sense, dreams work differently to everyday perception in that they foreground the play which, in waking life, makes meaning impossible. Dreams signify in ways which we either find impossible or unbearable, perhaps even unthinkable, in other forms of signification.

Understood as signification in this way, dreams cannot simply present the unconscious. That the unconscious can work within dreams becomes the *work* of the dream-work as displacement in the chain of signification. Here the imagined referent, which keeps the movement of signification at bay, is unhinged from it and the process of signification is allowed to slide. Any meaning for the dream, any truth imposed upon it, is only imposed retrospectively, and in this sense the dream is never literal or direct:

> It is true that in carrying out the interpretation in the waking state, we follow a path which leads back from the elements of the dream to the dream-thoughts and that the dream-work followed one in the

> contrary direction. But it is highly improbable that these paths are passable both ways. It appears, rather, that in the daytime we drive shafts which follow along fresh trains of thoughts and that these shafts make contact with the intermediate thoughts and the dream-thoughts are now at one point and now at another.
>
> (Freud 1900: 680)

Any truth imposed on the dream retrospectively arrests the play of signification of the dream-work and produces meaning in relation not to the dream, but rather to the truth by which the interpretation is produced.

In this sense, the dream-work is distinct from the text – the dream – and no longer has to reside in what happens in our psyches when we are asleep. Indeed, dream-*work* could also be at work for the subject in events or objects encountered in the everyday, even those as shocking and apparently incontrovertibly real as '9/11'. At the very least, we can no longer assume that it's not. What '9/11' is or was (even its time is uncertain) could in some ways be understood as putting the truth of the certainty of meaning into play, by returning to it the trace of its own dislocation from and to itself. In this way, that we struggle to impose meaning on the event retrospectively is no more than an effect of our own need to find ourselves at one with ourselves in it.[20] For Freud, this is always already impossible, but at the same time, the illusion of its possibility drives us on towards producing it because our own self-image necessitates that we do. What '9/11' means in these terms is crucial not only to making sense and restoring faith to the process of sense-making itself, but also to the interests of maintaining our collective sense of the truth of the cultural value by which that process has a use, *for us*. Our approach, or relation, to '9/11', then, is already predictably constituted in its value to us as individuals – what we find of our ego there – and collectively, in what we may find of the cultural values of the Law of the culture to which we submit in the process of becoming subjects of it. In this sense, the event '9/11' and the Ferrari Enzo are not too far removed from one another, at least at the level of their function and effect for us. *Any* object can produce the effect of disturbance in and for the subject, in its relation to it, regardless of any 'thing-in-itself-ness' to the object.

In addition to the dream-work understood in this way, Freud also remarked on a strange sort of textual effect at work within cultural texts that he argued gave rise, in certain circumstances, to feelings of something not being quite right. Something that is, which is out of joint, and not just in the text but also, perhaps more sharply, in the subject themselves in their relation to the text. This effect, which he termed 'the uncanny', thus became a focus for Freud in his further investigation of the status of objects for the subject in the subject–object relation.

In a single volume of the Penguin Freud Library – volume 14, *Art and Literature* – a number of Freud's works on aesthetics are collected together.

These include the elaboration of his idea of the parallels between the process of creative writing and daydreaming in producing an acceptable adult form of childish fantasy and wish fulfilment in and through art. They also include analyses of the author, characters and the subjects of texts, and the play of the illusion of the text in relation to the author as a guarantee of the ego. Like Nietzsche's concept of the value to culture of the illusion foregrounded by art, Freud seems to conceptualize art as a space in which socially unacceptable possibilities may be examined from a safe distance. However, it is Freud's work on the uncanny, as both textual effect and subject–object relation, which is of most interest to the project of cultural criticism underway here.

For Freud, the uncanny is not. That is to say, it is not present or integral either to itself or to the subject in whom the play of its trace may be felt. It comes not from the object or from outside of the object, but is rather generated from the complex interplay of the relation between the two as foundational to the constitution of each. As such, the uncanny can be thought of as a special case, what Freud calls 'the frightening':

> I will say at once that both courses lead to the same result: the uncanny is that class of the frightening which leads back to what is known of old and long familiar. How this is possible, in what circumstances the familiar can become uncanny and frightening, I shall show in what follows.
>
> (Freud 1990: 340)

In the first instance, '[s]omething has to be added to what is novel and familiar in order to make it uncanny' (1990: 341). The German term – *unheimlich* – carries with it the sense of unhomely not available in the English translation.[21] If something is unhomely, it is both reminiscent of home, of being *at home*, and of something which threatens that home and the subsequent feeling of being at home. That the home can be said in English to be where the heart is, suggests that the concept of home serves for the subject as a movable sense of where 'it' as ego is. This is, perhaps, how the concept of feeling at home works in common parlance. To the scene of this feeling, the *unheimlich* brings an unsettling feeling of deep disturbance to the subject's very sense of themselves. Like the dream-work, however, it is unlikely, for a variety of reasons, that either this feeling or its source will be present to the subject in any direct or literal way.

For Freud, there are, eventually, two kinds of unhomely effects: those which proceed from 'repressed complexes' (1990: 375) and so seem to mark something 'hidden and dangerous' (1990: 346) which can be resolved for the subject or surmounted; and those which proceed from the very ambivalence of the homely itself, which cannot be surmounted or resolved: 'Thus *heimlich* is a word the meaning of which develops in the direction of ambivalence, until it finally coincides with its opposite, *unheimlich*' (1990: 347).

While suggesting that the first class of the uncanny is most often the one found in art, Freud also insists that the second can never entirely be discounted:

> It would be more correct to take into account a psychological distinction which can be detected here, and say that the animistic beliefs of civilized people are in a state of having been (to a greater or lesser extent) *surmounted* [rather than repressed]. Our conclusion could then be stated thus: an uncanny experience occurs either when infantile complexes which have been repressed are once more revived by some impression, or when primitive beliefs which have been surmounted seem once more to be confirmed. Finally, we must not let our predilection for smooth solutions and lucid exposition blind us to the fact that these two classes of the uncanny experience are not always sharply distinguishable.
>
> (Freud 1990: 372)

The uncanny in Literature provides a more 'fertile province' for examination than the uncanny in 'real life' for Freud, since Literature can contain both the sense of the *unheimlich* and what he calls 'more besides' (1990: 372). Phantasy does not submit its content to reality testing, and so literature may produce many more uncanny effects than could reasonably be tolerated in real life.

The uncanny, in all of this, is not a thing in itself but rather a relation within which the play of the trace of the other within, the same is uncomfortably felt. That Literature, and by implication art, can serve both to foreground and to surmount the ambivalent disjunction of the *unheimlich* within the subject, makes the object a powerful site of cathexis. Here the object is over-invested by the subject in terms of itself, and this changes what the object is in its possible signification. It does not, however, allow for that object to be thought of as something in its own right, held in reciprocal relation to a subject in *its* own right. It can confirm and/or unsettle, and the work it performs in this direction will always be contingent (in space) and transient (in time).

Theories of the subject of culture as already estranged within itself as a very condition of becoming subject can, in some of the ways suggested here, provide analyses not available through the concept of the sublime. In particular, they can provide analyses which engage metaphysics by revealing the impossibilities always already entailed in what become both the possibilities of its foundation as such, and the radical impossibilities contained there. Here the case is made, not for a move beyond metaphysics – which in any case would now be impossible – but rather for a deconstruction of the terms by which metaphysics operates in order to demonstrate that it can never function absolutely to delimit the thinkable. That they do this not by recourse to either a something or a nothing outside of metaphysics, matters. It matters because it puts metaphysics itself into question, revealing as it does so, the ambivalence of the simultaneous impossibility of its own possibility. Abandoning metaphysics for something conceived of as outside metaphysics is always a risky business, since what is 'out there' will always be conceived in the terms by which we seek it.

The issue of aesthetics

Aesthetics, in the twists and turns depicted in this chapter, has a number of implications for critical practice. The issues raised by those twists and turns, however, may come to define what cultural criticism is and what it can do. Whether this is best thought of in terms of the sublime, of estrangement or of simulation, will both depend on the point of that practice, and in turn lead to a determination of what that practice can be. I have argued that this depends on a choice about how cultural criticism conceives of the subject–object relation. In these terms, the conclusion is that cultural criticism is better served by the function and effect of the concept of estrangement, than it is by that of the sublime or in different ways, by some understandings of the concept of simulation. If a critical engagement with the terms of the metaphysics it seeks to resist is the goal of cultural criticism, then it cannot achieve that by either standing outside of the terms of the constitution of that metaphysics as such, or by pointing to something else which does.

In addition, the issue of aesthetics, as I have stated it here, raises further questions – particularly about the real – which demand more detailed examination. That, however, must be deferred to another chapter yet to come.

More immediately, at least in terms of the development of the argument here, the issue of aesthetics gives rise to a question of ethics in relation to whether or not aesthetics can be understood either to have an ethical imperative, or to be 'properly' driven by one. By producing ethics on the scene of cultural criticism, it becomes possible to ask whether that criticism can, or should, develop in a relation to the ethical. Paradoxically, however, to state the issue in these terms is already to foreground the problem of any understanding of ethics as that which simply *is*.

3 Ethics

- Why ethics?
- The ethics of aesthetics
- The ethics of psychoanalysis
- The ethics of ethics
- The issue of ethics

Why ethics?

Can there be an ethics of anything in the sense of a single, universal framework through which particularities can be produced and judged? If such an ethics were possible, would it be desirable? And, without such a framework, is ethics even worth thinking about? These are just some of the questions which make ethics an issue for critical and cultural theory and, as such, a site upon which sometimes fierce critical disputes take place.

What is fixed under the sign of 'ethics', however, is not always made explicit in the different paradigms of cultural criticism it is called upon to serve. Ethics, it seems, can be apparent in a range of signifying practices from the seemingly mundane in the ethics of 'shopping', 'eating', 'writing', through the ethics of knowledge in 'the ethics of science', 'religion', 'critical theory', to the ethics of global practices in the ethics of 'engagement' (in war) 'international relations', and 'local government policy'. Yet quite what is constituted in these associations, even *ethically*, remains open to debate.

However, if ethics is to operate as more than simply that which a dominant or resistant force believes to be right, then what ethics can signify as well as what is at issue in the ways in which it can come to signify within critical and cultural theory, must be examined.

While it may not resolve the issue of ethics once and for all, what this chapter explores are the different frameworks for thinking about ethics – what it is and what it does – available to cultural criticism today. From the politics of representation in relation to race, gender and sexuality, through the different possibilities for the question of responsibility foregrounded by psychoanalysis, to the second order philosophical debate about how ethics can be ethical, the chapter engages a wide range of the terms through which ethics comes to operate in cultural criticism. This involves tracing ideas of the ethical from philosophical traditions as well as contemporary aesthetic practice, and thinking through what the consequences of each may be. In the end, rather than resolving the issue of ethics, the chapter argues that to do so would in itself be unethical.

The ethics of aesthetics

One of the foremost arenas of cultural criticism, in which ethics has been both constituted and mobilized, is that of aesthetics. From the explicit spiritual morality of Kant to the atheism of Nietzsche, the impact of art on subjects in the world has been invested by a notion of ethics as that which is either right or wrong. Underlying this constitution is a corresponding notion of art as representation, and as representation in address to both the world and subjects of that world. In the twentieth century, representation has been called to account for itself in these terms in as much as it has been analysed for the values it instigates and perpetuates. From accounts of language as 'man made', through those of the nineteenth-century novel as 'bourgeois' and of painting as a conservative form, to those of photography as fetishism, forms of representation have been scrutinized for, and judged in terms of, the 'fairness' of the picture of the world they represent.[1] This idea of an imperative for cultural criticism, not simply to appreciate the aesthetic beauty of its objects but rather to critically engage with the values generated from them, has to some extent founded cultural criticism as it was outlined in the Introduction. It is, then, vital to cultural criticism that its role is one of critique. The value of representation understood in this way also has implications for what can be perceived as its role in culture, raising questions about whether it should engage the world it represents by reflecting critically on it, to seek to change that world by representing it differently and so changing the way subjects of that world may come, habitually, to see it. One of the issues which has served to focus all these debates is that of 'positive representation', both in cultural practice and in cultural criticism itself.

The Black Arts Movement (BAM) in the United States of America, poses just these questions about the politics of representation and the role of a contestatory practice in relation to engaging that politics. Founded as it is on the basis of addressing and, thus *re*dressing the issue of race in the USA, it conceptualizes the function of representation in the world as one that inherently involves ethical choices. Aesthetics is not simply a matter of the beautiful here, but rather a contribution made to racism in America on the basis of forgetting of the politics of representation: 'The Black Arts Movement believes that your ethics and your aesthetics are one. That the contradictions between ethics and aesthetics in Western society is symptomatic of a dying culture' (*Ethics and Aesthetics* 2005: 1). What this statement most obviously implies is that one consequence of the forgetting it, points out is the decline of culture as a shared set of positive values. But it also implies that the decline of one culture can be arrested by an injection of a different set of values drawn from another. In the cultural project of BAM, 'Africa' comes to signify a grounding, not only for African-Americans, but also for the culture of America infused by the aesthetic sensibilities of African-Americans. The conception of representation at work in this serves to separate black Americans from Americans generally – to hold them in a hyphenated difference – and at the same time to reposition them within America as a vital cultural force. America may be revived from its cultural death throes, but only in acknowledgement of the value of a difference that comes from somewhere else. That difference is crucial, however, since it also serves to mark a force for change within that culture which will re-describe the place of African-Americans in it. Positive representation here is both positive for the self-image of the African-American subjects routinely discriminated against in American society and for the possibility of what American culture can be.

The conduit for both of these possibilities, as the broader project of BAM suggests, is the black subject in whose difference both the discrimination of American culture and the means of escape from that discrimination can be traced. Here subjectivity is understood to be positioned in a vital relation to representation on which, in part, it also depends. In these terms, growing up black in a culture within which being a citizen or even just a meaningful subject, is represented predominantly through the idealized figure of everyday white folk, damages self-perception.[2] Similarly, growing up black in a culture within which the most enduring representation of black people is that of 'Aunt Jemima' staring back at you from your pancakes, or of the black man as felon and the black woman as whore in the police mug shots ubiquitous in the daily news, makes identification of self-image (ego) in the sign of blackness in culture a hazardous daily process. It would be difficult to argue that these representations do not in some way matter to what it means to be a black subject in American culture today, or for that matter anywhere else, where being white is valued implicitly and unquestioningly.

Representation, understood as a particular form of relation between subjects in culture and the circulation of signs in that culture, comes to signify something much more than merely an incidental thing-in-itself. In something like a Freudian turn to the concept of an object *for* the subject in the subject–object relation explored in the previous chapter, representation comes to signify the possibility for subjects of recognition.

So, negative representation or absence of positive representation matters to the subject for whom representation provides the possibility of 'finding themselves there' in the recognition of an ego which is in turn confirmed by the finding. If we follow Freud, then that subject stands for *all* subjects. This clearly does not mean that subjects marked as other to that which operates as the 'normal' or 'right' in a culture – on the basis of the signification of, for example, the colour of their skin – are not subjects in any sense of the enculturation that term implies. What it does mean, however, is that maintaining a positive self-image in such a culture is more precarious.

However, while difference undoubtedly marks discrimination in ways that the Black Arts Movement outlines, it also provides the means by which that discrimination may be contested and redressed. Positive representation not only changes the object of identification for the subject constituted in difference, it also changes the difference upon which cultural discrimination depends. Representation thus becomes a potentially positive cultural force in engaging social and political regimes. Of course, representation does not spring from nowhere and the problem of the subject, as author in the representational process, returns to haunt the model thus described. If negative or absent representation of difference saturates the culture in which difference struggles to be its own thing-in-itself, then where does a sense of self, sufficiently positive in itself to change the dominance of negative representation, come from?

For the Black Arts Movement, it comes from the 'place' of another culture within which difference is differently distributed. Here the hyphenated African-American is held in the tension of identification with two cultural manifestations of the difference that the sign of black skin can signify. Africa, in this formulation, serves as a conceptual repository of positive signifying practices. And it is to the different cultural traditions of Africa, to the different sounds, textures and histories it comes to signify, that positive representation in this example turns. This model of representation, then, is one which enables a dual relation between representation, and the world of subjects it inevitably addresses. It functions simultaneously to produce difference and also to value that difference produced, as it must be, in the contingency of the chain of cultural values.

In the terms outlined by the Black Arts Movement, positive black representation becomes a matter of ethics by affirming 'the integral relationship between black art and black people' (*Ethics and aesthetics* 2005: 2). In the USA, this gives rise to black arts projects on the streets in Harlem as a means of shattering 'the illusions of the American body politic', and awakening 'black people to the meaning of their lives' (2005: 2). In this way, a concept of representation is linked to a conceptualization of the real, and both are linked to the structure of a world within which particular forms of discriminatory practice give rise to the denigration of particular forms of being within that world. Art is the means by which these practices can be contested and the values upon which they rest may be actively changed. In a sense, this begins to get to the nub of ethics as an issue which is inextricably linked to concepts of justice, legitimacy and something like freedom – the freedom to 'be' different, or to make another way of knowing circulate on the basis of that difference.

Of course, this is not only the province of something called 'black politics' but must be capable of operating everywhere where discrimination may be conceived of as such, and on behalf of a notion of 'the people' (variously constituted) as either 'oppressed', or 'devalued'. It is the same conceptual notion which, for example, also informs what have established themselves variously as 'feminist ethics' and 'gay ethics' among many possible others.

Feminist ethics, for example, depicts itself in 'an attempt to revise, reformulate, or rethink those aspects of traditional Western ethics that depreciate or devalue woman's moral experience' (*Stanford Encyclopedia of Philosophy* 2005: 1). In a 19-page entry to the *Stanford Encyclopedia of Philosophy*, this depiction continues by elaborating that western ethics 'shows little concern for women's as opposed to men's interests and rights', and that feminist ethics, by contrast, develops 'a wide-variety of women-centred approaches to ethics, including those labelled "feminine," "maternal," and "lesbian,"' (2005: 1) concluding that: 'Considered together the overall aim of all feminist approaches to ethics, irrespective of their specific labels, is to create a gender-equal ethics, amoral theory that generates non-sexist moral principles, polices and practices' (2005: 1). Feminist ethics, like those of the ethics of black aesthetics, seems here to reside in a contestatory practice within discriminatory systems of difference and the different possibilities for identification at work there. Again, feminist ethics situates such discrimination in a space delineated as 'the West', as an effect of the cultural values of its symbolic structures, and so as a rendering of certain constitutions of belonging within that space as less worthy than others. This time, however, the terms and conditions of that constitution are understood differently. Gender rather than race becomes the central marker of that discrimination, and the practice of renovating the metaphysics, which generates the difference through which such discrimination is possible, is posited as the necessary and urgent function of the ethics which ensues. While both conceptions do not necessarily exclude each other, each nonetheless foregrounds a particular source of resistant knowing, which in turn gives rise to a contestatory practice of representation in the interests of and on behalf of that source.

As a means of addressing power relations within culture, this is certainly attractive. But what does it make of ethics in its mobilization of the concept of ethics? Clearly, ethics here is a matter of *interest*, and as such is open to a variety of constitutions. In this sense of it, ethics is a value which is assumed, and thus left unexamined. Like truth in the preceding chapter, ethics functions to ground a particular way of knowing in a culture whose meanings appear to be fixed. While those meanings can be contested, the terms by which they arrive within culture are always already given. Contest, then, is always the contest of particular values *within* the system of meaning making that that system is. It is not necessarily, in other words, a contestation of the conditions of that system which make it systematic in the first place. In

Derrida's terms, we might suggest that this contestation works to redress or even to reverse the terms of particular power relations within metaphysics without necessarily engaging *the terms of* that metaphysics. If this is the case, then thought of conceptually in this way, ethics becomes a value generated by metaphysics within its own terms in order to guarantee its own continued function *as if it were real*. To paraphrase Nietzsche on truth, ethics is a value about which we have forgotten that that is what it is.

Positive representation as an aesthetic strategy and as a strategy of criticism has itself been contested in terms of its interest within the very groups it sets out to represent. What counts as 'positive', on what terms and in the service of which interests, has itself been hotly contested. In terms of what counts as 'positive' gender, sexuality and racialization, those contests have been about the terms of exclusion such categories perpetuate. For a film maker, such as Isaac Julien, what he terms the 'pressures of positive representation' themselves resist the limits of what representation, as signifying practice, can do. For Julien, meaning is more radically questioned by destabilizing the terms through which it is able to posit itself as value free in the first place. The film *Young Soul Rebels* (Julien 1991), for example, works to critique not just the power relations necessarily entailed in a violent relation between white and black in the year of the Queen's Silver Jubilee in Britain, but also within both the categories of 'black' and 'gender'. Here value is contested, but this time within the categories, as categories of a broader sense-making process.

Much of Julien's work – cinematically and theoretically – lends itself to another set of theoretical explorations which take place under the name of 'queer'. Queer, for resistant cultural practitioners, became a way of unsettling the terms of the categories by which metaphysics stabilizes itself as such. As a verb (to queer), queer can signify an action of putting 'out of joint', unsettling, destabilizing the very terms by which something comes to be something in the first place. As a verb, queer retains a sense of time which keeps it in motion conceptually and at least in principle prevents it from any form of grounding in a moment of its own 'now'. As a noun, however, queer comes to settle any movement promised by acting in reference to something outside of itself. It becomes a name (noun – nominal) whose referent is the thing-ness of dissonant sexual identity. In this sense, queer functions as a sign which, while it could be open to the play of signification, nonetheless arrests that play in the service of a given category. It too is interested and interesting and any ethics of queer in turn becomes grounded within the terms of that interest.

This notion of the possibilities and limits of an ethics based on a sense of the 'proper' function of representation in culture and its resistant politics is also apparent in the field of post-colonial studies. Here it raises fundamental questions not only about an imperative to put something into representation within a set of academic knowledges that had excluded it, but also about the very business of cultural criticism itself on the site of the post-colonial.

In an essay entitled 'Can the subaltern speak?' (Nelson *et al.* 1988: 271–316), the Bengali cultural critic Gayatri Chakravorty Spivak (1941 –) questions the practice of positive representation on different terms to those outlined by BAM, feminist ethics and queer, above. The question of the essay's title – of subalterneity and of speaking – is in some sense rhetorical, since the essay explores the terms by which either can be thought. From Gramsci's *Prison Notebooks* (1973), Spivak takes the term 'subaltern' which there had signified those subjects of culture whose value or importance is less than that of those who hold power and who subsequently come to wield that power over such subjects.[3] As a dissonant branch of historical research and knowledge, the project of subaltern studies is to return to history that which has been repressed – forgotten or marginalized – by the operation of history as an interested record of events.[4] Here that interest is that of an Indian elite concerned to produce an alternative to the English history of India which has been told in English terms. While focusing on a specific instance in which an ethics of representation is presumed, the essay has a wider significance within the debate about the ethics of aesthetics. It is significant because it questions, and in so doing unsettles, the very terms through which any claim for an ethics or a politics of representation are made. These terms, for Spivak, revolve around the referents of the subject of representation and the subject represented there. In her interrogation both of the concepts of the subject of representation and of the immediacy of speech, Spivak effectively deconstructs the ground on which positive representation seems comfortably settled. In this sense, what was merely assumed to be ethical in the former models becomes fundamentally unethical in Spivak's analysis.

As it operates within subaltern studies, the concept of the subaltern comes to designate those 'lived experiences' of groups of people constituted as powerless within society and thus overlooked or forgotten in that society. What Spivak questions is how we come to know what that is. In the most obvious sense, the subaltern is approached from the start in the terms of the *concept* of the subaltern. In this approach 'it' is already constituted as something outside of what it might, essentially, be and can only be understood in the terms of that something other than it. In this way, subaltern studies operates like simulation – producing the very thing it appears simply to 'find'. While this may be somewhat ameliorated in subaltern studies by the second term of Spivak's question, that term fares no better in her analysis of it. What, after all, is speech here presumed to be? For Spivak, speech functions conceptually as a direct manifestation of experience as though it were unstructured by the system of signification, and the power and values generated there. However, in her terms, any individual articulation in speech is possible in the first place only in terms of the communal system which language is. So, while the subaltern can literally speak, it can never do so within its own terms, particularly since those terms are those of the culturally marginalized and excluded. Combined with the approach that the concept subaltern makes, even if the subaltern can speak as such, subaltern studies will never 'hear' that speech except in anything other than those studies' own terms.

What Spivak questions here is in part the authenticity of the thing thus discovered. Authenticity is always impossible because it will always necessarily entail identification in terms other than itself. That is, in terms which automatically de-authenticate it. But Spivak's analysis also questions the theoretical gesture of essentializing the thing it sets out to speak on behalf of. What she points out is that what underlies any approach to the subaltern is the presumption of its being a thing-in-itself. This leads to a paradox which Spivak eventually seeks to resolve by advocating the practice of something she calls 'strategic essentialism'.[5] The paradox focuses the problem of analysing and contesting relations of power as they operate over a particular group of people, without at the same time perpetuating that power by analyses which arise within the terms by which that power constitutes itself as such. Spivak's 'way out'[6] of this paradox is to continue to utilize what she understands to be 'mistaken' conceptual terms, but to use them as if they were under erasure.[7] The concepts – of the subaltern, of speech, of the thing-in-itself – are thus grounding referents, but only temporarily and on the way to something else. This, for Spivak, is the only possible ethical move. It is one in which ethics is interested but also aware of that interest and so able to take it into account.

Strategic essentialism, however, is not the way out that Spivak desires. In the first place, the terms of the interest it marks are left unexamined. 'Strategic' is supposed to moderate the 'essentialism' to which it relates in the new binary pair. In some ways it does, since it creates a status for 'strategy' as a way of knowing – *as knowing better than* – the essentialism it associates itself with. In turn, 'strategy' itself should be open to contest – whose strategy, on behalf of whom, by whom and in what terms? Unless it is, strategy operates in the same way to ground the discourse announced in its name as that of truth. Here truth is not eternal, but nor is it true in itself. It is, as truth has always been, grounded by recourse to a further notion of transcendence. For Kant that was God, for Spivak it becomes 'the people', but both are problematic. In addition to this, while 'strategic' is supposed to modify 'essentialism' in the dual relation, so 'essentialism' is, by way of return, supposed to modify 'strategic'. Again, the question remains. On what basis can essentialism perform this modifying operation except by recourse to grounding in a referent of something outside of the system which generates it? Here, the strategic essentializer knows that there is no such thing-in-itself – 'the people' – but continues to act, for the moment, as if there is.

What holds all this together is itself grounded in knowing, and worse still in knowing better than that which it both seeks to contest and to act in the interests of. This can only be understood as ethics if what ethics signifies is the certainty of value embodied in the *knowing subject* who acts ethically by virtue of that knowing, and as 'knowing better than'.

This failure of strategic essentialism is in part an effect of its grounding in the concept of the knowing subject which operates in it without examination. But it also fails since it fails to take account of the involvement of ego in seemingly rational metaphysical processes. Here, 'knowing better than' does more than simply contest whatever powers that may be, it also restores the subject who knows – the strategizer – to itself in full confirmation of the completeness of that self.

What all of the formulations of ethics as a particular politics of representation lack, it would seem, is an account of the subject. Indeed, for ethics to mean more than the service of an interest or value which in turn is of interest to the subject for whom it serves, then the notion of the subject itself must be called to account. For that, ethics takes the turn into the field of psychoanalysis. As it turns out, this also entails an entirely different conceptualization of what representation is and what it does.

The ethics of psychoanalysis

What an account of subjectivity brings to the debate about ethics is primarily an account of self-interest as it operates on the scene of aesthetics, the politics of representation, and ultimately of psychoanalysis itself.

In a series of seminars for the Socíeté Française de Psychoanalyse conducted in Paris in 1959, the French psychoanalyst Jacques Lacan (1901–81) outlined some ideas of what ethics might be, what psychoanalysis might do that it could be thought of as ethical, and finally what the ethics of psychoanalysis, were it possible, might be constituted as. For Lacan, the sense of ethics explored in these seminars in turn emerges in relation to a series of concepts within his work as a whole, and it is worth attending to these in some detail here. These include 'desire', '**sublimation**', and what Lacan terms the 'tragedy' of the subject.

This 'tragedy' of the subject will emerge in the course of this chapter. Momentarily, however, it may be foregrounded by a paragraph in Lacan's introduction to the seminars on ethics where, what it is to be a subject in and of culture, is stated like this:

> The moral experience involved in psychoanalysis is the one that is summed up in the original imperative proposed in what might be called the Freudian ascetic experience, namely, that *Wo es war, soll Ich werden* with which Freud concludes the second part of his

> *Vorlesungen* (*Introductory Lectures*) on psychoanalysis. The root of this is given in an experience that deserves the term 'moral experience', and is found at the very beginning of the entry of the patient into analysis.
>
> That 'I' which is supposed to come where 'it' was, and which analysis has taught us to evaluate, is nothing more than that whose root we already found in the 'I' which asks itself what it wants. It is not only questioned, but as it progresses in its experience, it asks itself that question and asks it precisely in the place where strange, paradoxical, and cruel commands are suggested to it by its morbid experience.
>
> (Lacan 1999: 7)

Here 'experience' is that of finding oneself in the image of self which is always already other than itself. The 'I', already subject *of* and *to* the terms of the language system which generates the possible position 'I', is not authentically the 'I' of its own experience, since even if it 'knows' that experience, experience itself can only be represented within the possibilities that language allows. That Lacan can state the condition of the subject in these terms is an effect of his understanding of language as a system, and in that systematicity its role in constituting the subject.

This involves a partial reworking of Freud's thesis on the development of human being as it emerges into culture. For Lacan, the subject is not born but made. The raw material of this making is the little animal of human being which, while it has the potential to become a part of the culture it inhabits, is not yet ready to do so in its raw state. It is in this sense, like the raw eggs of an (h)omme-lette which Lacan jokingly makes it an analogy to: the raw human animalism must be cooked in order to make it palatable to culture. In order to do this, the human infant must make a move from the realms of its being into the realms of meaning. It must, in other words, give up being for meaning. This move, once made, separates the human from its being and it can never return to the state of *being outside of meaning* except, ironically, in death. Death is ironic here since we can never experience our own death. By definition, if 'I' am here (as a subject in meaning), then death is not. If death is here (as a particular state of organic being), then 'I' am not. For Lacan, you can have being *or* meaning, but you cannot have both (Figure 3.1).[8]

One way in which it is possible to understand the import of this move from being into meaning, is in relation to Saussure's conceptualization of language as a signifying system. For Saussure, language as a system refers only to itself. In this sense, not only does it precede 'us' in the sense that it is there before us – we 'join' or acquire it – but it also has, by virtue of that precedence, no *relation to* us. Even the position of the 'I', the most seemingly personal of all signs in language, does not pertain specifically to me. At the very least, it is communal since the position it appears to delineate is shared by everyone else who identifies themselves there. If and when we move from being into meaning in Lacan's terms, then, we do so only in meaning's terms and so emerge as *subject to* those terms and as *subjects of* them.

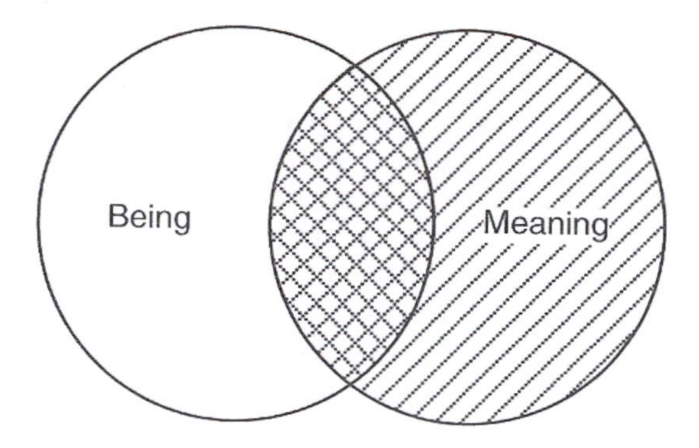

Figure 3.1 Being and meaning for Lacan

That we imagine it otherwise, is also an effect of the operation of language for Lacan. Here language works on the basis of a promise. What it promises is a place for being within meaning. However, since the move from being into meaning involves a radical separation of being from itself as such, meaning becomes a place of loss, and the promise cannot be kept. This is one sense of the 'tragedy' of the subject for Lacan. If it is a tragedy, however, it is one which, for the subject's sense of itself at least, is quickly recuperated. The loss that meaning entails is recuperated for the subject within another of the realms that Lacan conceives of as constitutive of subjectivity – that of the imaginary.

The function of the imaginary, in Lacan's schema of the subject, is to mask the loss that is entailed in the foundation of the subject through the production of fantasies within which it can come to seem as if it is whole. However, while fantasy appears to make up for the lack by covering the absence signified there, it too can do so only in the terms of, and in relation to, the processes of signification of which language is a part. In this sense, the subject which emerges in language is aided and abetted by the imaginary to which it also gives rise. This aiding and abetting is focused for Lacan in the metaphor of the mirror stage, which, he argues, forms a rehearsal for the development of the subject in its entry into language.

Occurring at a stage in an infant's development before its position in language has quite been achieved, the mirror stage relates to that process by rehearsing the division of the psyche which will take place there. For Lacan, the metaphor of the mirror is significant since we appear to find there a passive reflection of ourselves. In this conception, the self that looks and the self that is seen appear to be at one with each other, although by logical necessity the self of the observer must at least be imagined to *be there* prior to the observation in order to make it. While we may check ourselves in a mirror, then, the self we check for is presumed to already be there. The glance in the mirror seems merely to be one of confirmation, albeit an anxious one.

But as Lacan observes, even in this presumption of a coincidence between the observer and the observed, there are still two parties, not merely one. That these parties can be brought together is an effect of a process of *identification*. In this sense, the passive act of appearing simply to see myself in a mirror is transformed into an active relation of identification of myself with the image that 'I' – as a result of that identification – find there.

For Lacan, the mirror is a metaphor for the process of self-perception as a process of self-identification, which he seeks to explore. In this sense, it is not finally about looking in actual mirrors, although it may of course include that. The realization dramatized by the metaphor is the relation of identification for the subject in something outside of itself – what Lacan terms the '**Imago**', or idealized image of self presented to the ego. In which case, the mirror could be the other – as in the parent who appears to recognize me as I see myself. However, as we all know from suffering the persistent teenage anguish of having parents/bosses/lovers who don't understand us, such recognition is at best fraught. When the parent 'recognizes' the child in these terms, s/he doesn't simply recognize it for what it is – in the terms of its own idealized image of itself – but rather in relation to terms that belong to the parent. The recognition of self, available in the gaze of the parent thus understood is conditional upon the terms within which it is offered. I can constitute a sense of myself there, but only by submitting the self found to the terms that that 'recognition' demands. Furthermore, for the subject to continue to recognize itself in the gaze of the other, it must disavow the dialectical process of the gaze itself. Not to do so would be psychotic in the sense that a very sense of self – 'that's me!' – depends upon it. In this sense, the apparent recognition of self is for Lacan a fundamental **misrecognition**, since all that is recognized is a place within the symbolic order to which the subject – as the price of that sense – subjects itself in the process of becoming a subject in meaning. I am a subject for the other, as the other signifies other people or objects.

While language, as an aspect of what Lacan now calls the symbolic, and *misrecognition*, as an operation of the fantasy of self-recognition, each play a role in the constitution of the subject, however, they do not do so alone. The imaginary and the symbolic work together, albeit in different ways, in producing the subject as an effect of the confluence of the two. Conceptually, the subject emerges here as an effect of the interplay of the imaginary and the symbolic, rather than as any source of origin for them. But if the subject is an effect of confluence in this way, that confluence must also include, at least for Lacan, the additional pressure of the real from which the being of the now subject of meaning has been radically separated. The subject, in Lacan's terms, is therefore an effect of the tripartite imaginary, symbolic and real (Figure 3.2).

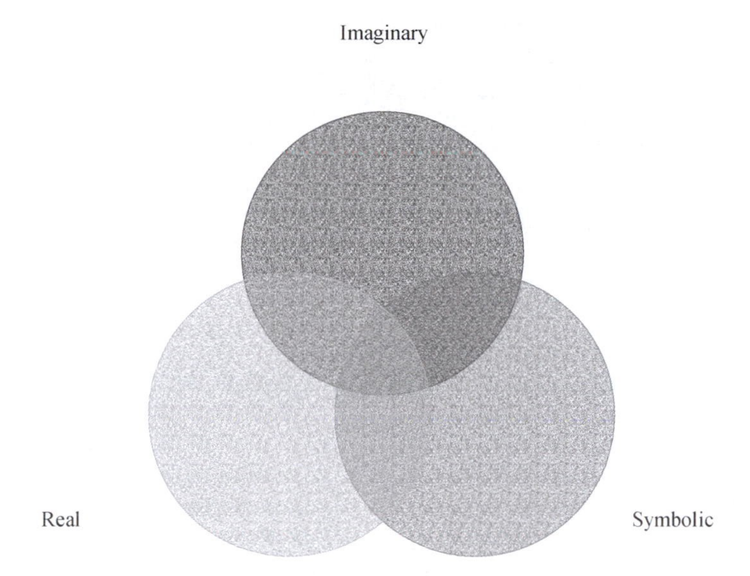

Figure 3.2 Lacan's imaginary, symbolic and real

Here, in Figure 3.2, the three realms of the imaginary, symbolic and real, as both distinct yet related and at the same time involved with one another, can be perceived by virtue of their representation in the form of the Venn diagram. But this does not capture the entirety of what Lacan constitutes as the confluence which constitutes the subject. To the Venn diagram of the tripartite structure, then, we may add the topology of the borromean knot – a knot which has no beginning and no end. Here, in Figure 3.3, it becomes impossible to trace for the confluence a proper inside or outside, since the knot has no point of origin within itself nor point of arrival. It is, as a knot, a continuous thread.

Importantly, without the confluence thus stated, the subject could not be what it is, or operate in culture as it does, for Lacan. But then, neither could the imaginary, the symbolic or the real operate as they do without the simultaneous implication of each within the others. In this way, Lacan negotiates the conceptual trap of a subject constituted either in absence or presence, inside or outside, since it is never fully within, or a possibility of either one or the other of the realms which compose it.

Just as we appear to find ourselves within the image held out in the gaze of the other, so we appear to find ourselves in the act of identification in

Figure 3.3 The borromean knot

language which the pronoun of the 'I' seems to provide by standing in for us there. In Lacan's analysis of the misrecognition entailed in the appearance of the recognition, however, both processes of founding the subject are also precarious. If my ego depends for being itself on the gaze of an other which sustains that illusion, then it is, from the start, in thrall to that gaze. Worse, that gaze is itself entailed in the necessary process of sustaining the illusion of yet another subject's imago and all of its demands in relation both to recognition and to signifying in meaningful terms.

When the interests of both appear to converge, something like harmony may momentarily appear to be achieved. This is in part what 'love' is for Lacan – appearing to find oneself as oneself in the gaze of another for whom the appearance of finding themselves there is reciprocally confirmed. The moment the cost of that reciprocation entails a perceived curtailment or lack of recognition of that self in the terms that self (as imago) necessitates, then the harmony once 'felt' as love can be transformed into that of the discordance felt as 'hate'. Here what is felt symbolically as hate, comes entirely from within the subject as a meaningful sign of the discord that founds it. Once it emerges as a sign in this sense, it is also immediately disavowed, deflected out from the space of the subject who 'feels' it onto the inadequacies or lack within the other. The ego, in this sense, is never *finally* present for Lacan. Lacking, dependent and an effect of misrecognition, it is always striving to maintain itself, defending itself against everything which threatens to undo it. In this sense, what Lacan terms 'paranoiac alienation' results from 'the deflection of the specular I into the social I' (2003: 6).[9]

The tragedy of the subject in this second sense of it, is the tragedy of its foundation on the basis of a relational process within which it is inevitably lost to the process itself. For Lacan, this is the basis for an analysis of the aggression of the **superego**, particularly as it pertains to the other in the dialectical process of dependency that subjectivity becomes.[10] But the other understood in these terms is also not the only other there is for Lacan. Distinguishing between the little other 'o' (or 'a' in the French 'autre') and the big Other 'O', Lacan distinguishes between other people or objects and the symbolic structures of culture. The symbolic is the *big* Other, in the sense that it is not dependent on any form of relation with the subject. While I might behave in certain ways, in order to *be for* the little other – I might not swear in front of my Dad – language cares nothing of my sense of self in relation to it, since it does not depend in turn on any form of recognition from me. Language does not need me in order to be the system of signification it is, since that is merely the generation of signs systematically. Any value generated in that system is, of course, a value in relation to subjects, but that is merely an effect of the system, rather than its origin or its capacity to be the system, as understood by Saussure.

In this lies a further sense of loss in the foundation of subjectivity. If language is merely a system of signs, then any recognition the subject finds there, is open to the effect of the movement of the sign as an effect of signification. Understood systematically, as we saw in Chapter 1, the sign is empty, its meaning generated syntagmatically and paradigmatically by difference and association. Here, difference is also deferral, since what any given sign can signify, will depend on what comes before and after it in the chain of signification. Meaning, even if we conceive of it as being temporarily within the sign, is still never either fully present or absent there. This does not necessarily mean that signs never signify anything, merely that what they signify is an effect strung out in a potentially limitless process of difference and deferral. That the subject appears to find itself in the signs of a language system, means that even there its presence, as subject, is unstable, even impossible. The subject is destined, for Lacan, to be constituted in the endless process of difference and deferral that meaning is, and so endlessly to seek there what it will never find once and for all: the ***petit objet a*** which promises to end the movement of desire, by making good the loss on which it is founded. A Ferrari, a new lover, or even an understanding of Lacan, might do it temporarily but once achieved, the meaning apparently found there will itself be subject again to the endless difference and deferral that meaning ultimately is.

That does seem tragic. It might go some way towards rationalizing a certain perception of Lacan's theory of the subject as pessimistic. If it is pessimistic, however, it is only pessimistic in relation to a certain conceptualization of the subject as a presence capable of eluding the curtailment of the fullness of its presence which is threatened by something other than the subject itself – capitalism, racism, 'the system' or the 'monstrous other'. That is not necessarily tragic. Indeed, it may even open up further possibilities for ethics in analyses of oppression, and aggression with which ethics comes to concern itself.

Conceptualized in Lacan's terms, 'the system' and 'the monstrous' are fully within the subject whose existence, as such, depends radically upon them. The consequences of this for thinking about 'the other' in cultural criticism are vast, and they will be examined further in the following chapter on alterity. In the context of the discussion of ethics underway here, however, we may say that any concept of ethics itself necessarily entails, and is dependent upon, a concept of the other as other than self, conceived of as presence. That is, fully present to itself. For ethics to mean more than merely the service of an interest, as was argued in the context of the ethics of aesthetics above, then that interest – the terms and conditions by which something is served – must be subjected to further critique. What Lacan's formulation of subjectivity offers is not just the critique of interest as value, but also that of interest as the interest of the subject in the action of critiquing it. What is invested, we might now ask, in the act of grounding our actions or non-actions within the world and the meanings generated by them for the subjects who do the grounding in the first place? What happens to ethics when we begin to think it within these terms?

For Lacan, the answer is that there are two different sorts of consequences. One is the possibility of an ethics of psychoanalysis; the other the possibility of ethics as something which can never be grounded in the service of meaning and certainly not in relation to the ego. The first possibility is reasonably clear in Lacan's formulation of what psychoanalysis can be and of what it can do. It is, as the quotation which began this section states – the 'morality' proposed by Freud's 'original imperative': 'Wo es war, soll Ich werden' (Lacan 1999: 7). Where it was, so 'I' shall come to be.[11] Or, as Lacan puts it:

> That 'I' which is supposed to come where 'it' was, and which analysis has taught us to evaluate, is nothing more than that whose root we already found in the 'I' which asks itself what it wants. It is not only questioned, but as it progresses in its experience, it asks itself that question and asks it precisely in the place where strange, paradoxical, and cruel commands are suggested to it by its morbid experience.
>
> (Lacan 1999: 7)

The point of psychoanalysis for Lacan is not to mask this radical disjunction of the subject, 'its sole goal the calming of guilt', and so restore to it an illusion of harmony within which the 'defiles of the signifier' may be abolished (2003: 342). Rather, it is to accept that that subject defiled by the signifier, disjointed and self-interested, is the only subjectivity we can possibly have. The ethics of psychoanalysis, then, is an ethics which does not serve to tame, to mask, or to deny the operation of the ego – since we can never be sure of any lack of interest in which we might believe we have transcended its reach – but rather to face it for what it is and to take it into account.

For Lacan, this matters in the sense that the motivations of the subject thus constituted are never pure. It matters for the ethics of representation in that what can be claimed to be spoken on behalf of the other, or even the authentic self of dissonant experience, is never simply un-invested. There's always something in it for the subject that constitutes itself as dissonant, or speaking on behalf of an other. And that, while it seems otherwise, is always the interest of self-interest. At the end of the mirror stage essay, Lacan sums up the significance of his theories of the aggressivity of the subject by writing:

> At this juncture of nature and culture, so persistently examined by modern anthropology, psychoanalysis alone recognizes this knot of imaginary servitude that love must always undo again, or sever.
>
> For such a task, we place no trust in altruistic feeling, we who lay bare the aggressivity that underlies the activity of the philanthropist, the idealist, the pedagogue, and even the reformer.
>
> (Lacan 2003: 8)

What he suggests here is not only that the subject is always motivated by the aggression of an ego in defense of itself, but that this 'always' is never more insidious than in acts of seeming selflessness performed by subjects for others. In these terms, it is not just that there is always something in it for the subject that can be construed in financial or material ways. While the organizers and performers involved with the event that was Live 8, for example, benefited from the increased record sales it brought about, they also benefited more fundamentally from an investment of the ego there.[12] There was something else that was in it for them in finding a sense of themselves in the image of self available to them there, and, as such, something that was much more fundamental than anything else that could be more readily identified. Recognizing one's self in the image of selflessness that working on behalf of the other seems to constitute for it there, is in Lacan's terms, as entirely invested by ego as an apparently selfish recognition of self-interest can be said to be. The difference is one of masquerade. This is the masquerade of the ego not to be where it is, or of the subject to be where the ego is not. And this applies to all subjects at all times. There is no giving which is not also always already a form of self-interest.

If we think of this in terms of the millions spent on the Judaeo-Christian festival of Christmas, for example, what's at stake there might become clear. Every year people spend more money than they can afford on gifts which often, though not always, have very little to do with the wishes of those they are given to. It's better to give than to receive, we think as the cash seeps away. But why is it better? In Lacan's terms, it's better because what we buy is the identification of self with the illusion of giving to the other without want of return, that the gift we give comes to signify for us. What is at stake here then is the illusion, however fleeting, of the satisfaction of the ego sublimated in the masquerade by which it can be free of the guilt of self gained at the expense of the other. In Lacan's terms, giving therefore always entails an act of aggression, albeit masked, towards the other.

The second possibility of ethics is already implicit within the terms of the first and may be approached in Lacan by way of a statement which he later made about the status of psychoanalysis itself. Writing on the 'Subversion of the subject and the dialectic of desire in the Freudian unconscious' in 1960, Lacan argued that analysis of the subject did not in turn necessitate sovereignty either of the subject or for the framework which de-institutes the sovereignty of that subject:

> Let us set out from the conception of the Other as the locus of the signifier. Any statement of authority has no other guarantee than its very enunciation, and it is pointless for it to seek it in another signifier, which could not appear outside this locus in any way. Which is what I mean when I say that no metalanguage can be spoken, or, more aphoristically, that there is no Other of the Other. And when the Legislator (he who claims to lay down the Law) presents himself to fill the gap, he does so as an imposter.
>
> (Lacan 2003: 343–4)

Any metalanguage, any Law which claims to come from somewhere other than language as cultural value and so to be capable of laying down that Law as a guarantee of meaning which is not also involved in the very terms of that meaning itself, is false. It is also paradoxical in that it shows itself to be false in the very act of its attempted intervention.

If there is no Other of the Other in these terms, then any claim to ethics will itself always already be invested by the very terms that make ethics meaningful in the first place. Ethics, understood as such, can never be ethical in the sense of residing somewhere outside of the system – of cultural value, of language, of the ego – in a place of innocent transcendence. Claims made for ethics supposedly by the ethical in this way are always the claims of an imposter.

This second sense of ethics as always already invested with the self-interest of the subject, is for Lacan, where any possibility for ethics stops. The best we can do is to foreground the self-interest necessarily entailed in thinking ethics and by foregrounding it, take it into account. This taking of the ego into account, in any conception of ethics, is also explored in philosophical terms by Jacques Derrida in his account of the gift. However, there the possibility of banishing the ego from the scene of ethics becomes an imperative if there is to be a possibility of ethics at all. An ethics devoid of the ego for Derrida is the possibility of what he comes to term, an 'ethics of ethics'.

The ethics of ethics

For Derrida, however differently he may arrive at the proposition, there is also no such thing as a gift:

> *At the limit, the gift as gift* ought not *appear as gift: either to the donee or to the donor*. It cannot be gift as gift except by not being present as gift. If the other perceives or receives it, if he or she keeps it as gift, the gift is annulled. But the one who gives it must not see it or know it either; otherwise he begins, at the threshold, as soon as he intends to give, to pay himself with a symbolic recognition, to praise himself, to give back to himself symbolically the value of what he thinks he has given or what he is preparing to give.
>
> (Derrida 1994: 14)

The gift here is always impossible not only because it is invested by the narcissism detailed by Lacan but also because, conceptually, it is the site of an impossible contradiction. In order to be a gift, the gift must constitute itself as a thing-in-itself with no remainder to be filled or absorbed by anything outside of itself. Here, the act of giving entailed in the gift as 'gift-in-itself' would also have to be giving as a form of expenditure without either reserve or excess. Without reserve, expenditure must expend itself entirely to the point where no further expenditure is possible. In order to give, the gift must *give itself* entirely and so disappear from itself as such. Any recognition of the gift *as gift* immediately annuls it.

This has consequences for the possibility of the gift itself but also, of course, for the subject necessarily entailed in the act of giving. In order not to be the imposter, detailed by Lacan, the subject that gives in Derrida's terms would also have to give itself entirely in the act of giving and so expend itself with no thought of return. For Lacan, this is impossible, since such giving entails the disappearance of the subject from itself. No matter how much I am prepared to give to Oxfam, I am in no sense prepared to give myself in my own expenditure as such to the other which Oxfam represents. If this means maintaining an implicit aggressivity towards the other, then so be it. If I can't erase that aggressivity except in self-expenditure, then I'll just have to find better ways of disavowing the aggressivity entailed in the act, in the interests of self-preservation. And I do. However, any thought that this doing entails giving – of the gift as Derrida conceives of it – is always already annulled. It is always already the masquerade of an imposter.

Without the gift as expenditure without either reserve or return, for Derrida there can be no ethics. At least there can be no ethics which is not already the masquerade of the imposter. In these terms, wherever ethics is claimed, what is constituted there is destined to be unethical in ethics' terms, since it already appears within a conceptual framework for deciding what ethics is. For Derrida, as long as it operates within the terms of metaphysics as though those terms were self-sufficient, ethics can only ever be ethical in the terms of that metaphysics. Thought as ethics, then, ethics cannot be ethical. This poses a problem about the possibility of ethics and in what terms ethics may posit itself as such.

For Derrida, while metaphysics is all we have, it is never the coherent absolute it seems. If cultural criticism engages with metaphysics critically, the ambiguities, impossibilities and radical incommensurability of its logic, in short, its **aporias**, can be revealed. Importantly, these are aporias which emanate not from outside of metaphysics, which is impossible in Derrida's terms, but rather *within* it. The terms and conditions by which metaphysics operates, always produce that metaphysics as inevitably unsettled and incomplete, even to itself. As long as we approach metaphysics as though it were finally settled, then the values produced there will always be those which are recuperable in terms of that metaphysics and which serve to sustain it in its own apparent totality. If, on the other hand, we approach it from within its terms as though it were not complete to itself, a different set of possibilities can follow.

Totality, for Derrida, is not only undesirable – *wherever* it may be found or invoked – it is also impossible. That it seems possible is merely an effect of a forgetting in relation to its contingency. Moreover, totality is impossible in the very conditions of its possibility in the first place. This is to say that the terms by which totalities are produced as possible, are also the conditions by which their impossibility is simultaneously made possible. An effect of difference and deferral, the concept 'totality' is itself as open to the same play of differance (with an 'a') which founds and unsettles it, as any other.

In the essay 'Differance', Derrida approaches differance as a 'silent tracing' of the other within the self same rather than as a thing-in-itself:

> The first consequence ... is that differance is not. It is not a being-present, however excellent, unique, principal or transcendent one makes it. It commands nothing, rules over nothing, and nowhere does it exercise any authority. It is not marked by a capital letter. Not only is there no realm of differance, but differance is even the subversion of every realm. This is obviously what makes it threatening and necessarily dreaded by everything in us that desires a realm, the past or future presence of a realm. And it is always in the name of a realm that, believing one sees it ascend to the capital letter, one can reproach it for wanting to rule.
>
> (Derrida 1973: 153)

Not only does differance here not function as a thing, it also threatens the logical metaphysical possibilities of any 'thing' that might be instituted in its name. It marks the conditions of the possibility of the thing as always already impossible as a thing in its own right, even in the moment in which that possibility is produced.

It is here, in the play of differance thus described, that Derrida finds what he calls the 'hope' of an ethics of ethics 'at least in this world' (Borradori 2003: 114–6). Constituted in the play of differance as a trace of the other within the self same, ethics can be opened to the radical uncertainty of its own foundation, and in this the 'matter of strategy and risk' as 'strategy without finality' (Derrida 1973: 135) may be glimpsed. Just as there is no Other of the Other for Lacan, so there can be no totality in the sense of a Metaphysics of Metaphysics for Derrida. What there can be for Derrida, however, is the differance of metaphysics and thereby of any totality which gets to function as though it were complete to itself.

In these terms, we may understand an ethics of ethics not as a meta-ethics (more ethical than thou) but rather a set of procedures through which something other than a totality of ethics as a logical metaphysical possibility may be traced. One of these procedures may entail the refusal of the decision in terms of the ethics that posits itself as such. Another, related to the first, is to reveal the inevitable play of the trace within the terms by which ethics appears to know itself.

For Derrida, there are no universals, or at least none that are universal in the sense of being complete to themselves. Indeed, the very opposition universal/particular is itself a totalizing gesture which is always already impossible. In Derrida's sense of differance, the particular will always play within the universal and the universal within the particular, since the possibility and impossibility of each are dependent upon the other. The trace of the other will always trace the oppositions constituted in these terms, not as a presence in itself but rather as the play of the movement of that opposition in both the space and the time of difference. While the constitution of the universal may seem to depend upon expelling the other of the particular, it can never quite fully manage either to expel that other from its terms or to manage its effects within itself. If we begin the task of thinking the particular within the universal, and vice versa, then any instance of either can be shown to be invested by the trace of its other. In these terms, any appearance of a universal – of freedom, terror, right, for example – can be shown not merely to be culturally relative but, more devastatingly, radically dependent on the trace of the other it seeks to master. Here, any mobilization of the principle of universality will always be enacted in a moment of what Derrida terms 'singularity', which will constitute that universal in an uncertain relation to its terms. Understanding this play of differance is where 'hope' for ethics as yet to come, may rest for Derrida.[13]

Writing in *The Gift of Death* in 1996, Derrida sets about the task of working through the possibilities of the play between the universal and the singular in notions of 'the gift', 'responsibility', and 'obligation', already at play in the broader scope of his writing. In the title, *The Gift of Death*, the ambiguity of the French verb 'donner' plays across the noun 'mort' in a way which associates the two and at the same time foregrounds that association. To give can mean in the French of 'donner' both 'to give' and 'to put to death'. This is significant since the analysis of responsibility which happens in the name of the book maintains the irreducible paradox to which its title points. *The Gift of Death* is a complex work involving discussion of a variety of significant issues in critical theory, not the least of which is the possibility of justice. In order to illustrate something of the paradox of ethics, as he conceptualizes it, it may be worth briefly exploring here just one of the analogies Derrida gives. In his readings of the texts of philosophy and theology for the possibilities of justice they may release or close off, Derrida produces a particular reading of the Judaeo-Christian-Islamic story of the sacrifice of Isaac.[14]

In the Genesis story, Abraham is instructed by God to sacrifice his dearly beloved son Isaac. God, as an absolute, has spoken in the form of the command to Abraham which Abraham, if he is to demonstrate his faith in that absolute, must be obliged to fulfil. On the surface of things, the act is not only excruciating for Abraham – he must destroy the thing he most loves to prove his love of God – but it also makes no sense to him. Derrida writes of this:

> Abraham comes to hate those closest to him by keeping silent, he comes to hate his only beloved son by consenting to put him to death [*lui donner la mort*]. He hates them not out of hatred, of course, but out of love. He doesn't hate them any less for all that, on the contrary. Abraham must love his son absolutely to come to the point where he will grant him death, to commit what ethics would call hatred and murder.
>
> (Derrida 1996: 65)

For Abraham to fulfil his obligation to the absolute other of God, he must act against what seems merely to be right for him, and as he can conceive of it as right in the world of values he inhabits. He must, in other words, give himself up to the principle of an other in the absolute otherness of that other. Here the absolute other must, in order to be absolutely other, remain beyond Abraham's grasp. Nonetheless, he must trust to it all the same. In order to do so, Abraham must sacrifice the thing which is most precious to him without being able to rationalize the sacrifice in terms of himself. Thus, the sacrifice he is called upon to make annuls itself the moment it is understood in Abraham's terms. For the sacrifice to remain as sacrifice, he cannot kill Isaac out of hate (I never liked him anyway) or out of motivation (God's love is worth more) only out of obligation to the principle of absoluteness for which God stands. With differance in mind, such absoluteness is also such only in the moment of the singularity of any manifestation of it.

While this parable works for Derrida, in the singularity of his analysis of it, as an approach to the possibility of an ethics of ethics, it remains of course a parable. For cultural criticism, the question which arises from this reading of what ethics might become is what strategies it might open up to it, even while acknowledging that such strategies are always 'in the end', strategies 'without finality' in the singular moment of its own 'now' (1973: 135).

Taking '9/11' as one of the potent signs in our times, Derrida argues, in a later set of dialogues, that we may trace the possibilities for ethics there. In response to the implicit question of how critical and cultural theory may respond to '9/11', Derrida proposes a series of strategies by which both it and the cultural criticism which approaches it, may be understood.

In the first place, Derrida asserts that we do not as yet 'know' '9/11', since it does not appear in itself as a single thing-in-itself, but rather as a series of interrelated policies and procedures which are inevitably traced within it and of which it is the trace:

> When you say 'September 11' you are already citing, are you not? ... We do not in fact know what we are saying or naming in this way: September 11, *le 11 septembre*, 11 September. The brevity of the appellation (September 11, 9/11) stems not only from an economic or rhetorical necessity. The telegram of this metonymy – a name, a number – points out the unqualifiable by recognizing that we do not recognize, or even recognize that we do not yet know how to qualify, that we do not know what we are talking about.
>
> (Borradori 2003: 85–6)

We do not know what we are talking about in the name of the sign '9/11' because, for Derrida, we do not know the potentially limitless detail by which that sign is itself traced. This detail might include 'knowing' the detail of the historical specificities of 'democracy', 'freedom', 'terror', as well as those of 'economy' and 'circulation', particularly in relation to 'oil' and 'land', even 'kingdoms'. But the traceable, as an effect of the constitution of '9/11' in the moment of its singularity, will not be exhausted there. To acknowledge even the possibility of such detail, is to recognize that what is the sign '9/11' is nowhere complete in *any* account of it – even, and perhaps most especially, Derrida's.

Another implication to which examination of the parable gives rise for Derrida is that while we must accept that what the sign '9/11' appears to signify is loaded by any account which produces it, the invitation to decide – in the interests of right or wrong, international security, the good of the people, and so on – must also be refused. For Derrida, there are never 'sides' as such, except as they may be produced in the service of one or the other:

> On no side is the logic of sovereignty ever put into question (political sovereignty or that of the nation-state – itself of onto-theological origin, though more or less secularized in one place and purely theological and non-secularized in another): not on the side of the nation-states and the great powers that sit on the Security Council, and not on the other side, or other sides, since there is precisely an indeterminate number of them.
>
> (Borradori 2003: 111)

Sovereignty here, is that which must be resisted and de-instituted no matter the rationality of interest it serves. In this sense, the strategy (as the 'risk' that Derrida acknowledges yet urges analysis to take) would be to resist any and all sovereignty – of the subject, the state, the ontological, the theological, the onto-theological – no matter where it reigns – in the cause, the ethnic, the powerless, and so on. It is not unless and until these conditions, of knowledge and of the de-institution of the sovereignty of sovereignty are exhausted, that an ethics of ethics can begin to appear, and then only as a possibility. That those conditions are not there for us in the moment of our 'now' does not mean that we cannot work towards producing them. This is at times counter-intuitive, since the imperative to 'do something about it, now' overwhelms another imperative to bring about the possibility of a different set of conditions. It is in this second imperative, however, that Derrida finds his 'hope'.

One immediate site within which we may work towards such hope is, for Derrida, that of the United Nations as an institution of International Law. While exploring the possibilities of this site, however, Derrida is under no illusions that what the United Nations is, is thoroughly invested by, if not founded upon, the very interests he seeks to deconstruct. For Derrida, in his approach to the parable of the demand of the sacrifice of Abraham, the possibilities for world relations can be read. In the Bible of course, the absolute of God is invested by the theological conditions of the faiths that produce it. So too are the responses available to us today in relation to '9/11' invested both by the theology and ontology of their hyphenated association. But, if we could divest our thinking of its onto-theological conditions, could we be left with the play of a non-onto-theological singularity within and across a different kind of universal? If we could, then such a universal would have to be thought of as a 'restricted economy' in the sense outlined in the differance essay. As such, it would have nothing to do with *any* form of 'thing' locatable outside of the system itself. In that earlier essay, Derrida writes:

> I have tried elsewhere, in a reading of Bataille, to indicate what might be the establishment of a rigorous, and in a new sense 'scientific,' *relating* of a 'restricted economy' – one having nothing to do with an unreserved expenditure, with death, with being exposed to non-sense, etc. – to a 'general economy' or system that, so to speak, takes account of what is unreserved.
>
> (Derrida 1973: 151)

Taking all of this into account, Derrida turns for such a universal to Law, not as an end in itself but rather as a possible absolute which is, in its singularity, *absolute*. Just as language, understood as system, refers only to itself in Lacan's analysis of the subject in language, so Law may be understood as a system to refer only to itself. It need care nothing of the values it intervenes within. In this sense, Law may operate as the absolute obligation to act in its terms without recourse to either understanding or rational interest as we may conceive of them in the singularity of our 'now'. So long as Law could be Law – for *all* at *all* times regardless of momentarily apparent particular consequences for interests that attempt to associate to it – then something like an ethics of ethics may be possible:

> Everyone will no doubt point to existing international law (the foundations of which remain, I believe, perfectible, revisable, in need of recasting, both conceptually and institutionally). But this international law is nowhere respected. And as soon as one party does not respect it the others no longer consider it respectable and begin to betray it in their turn. The United States and Israel are not the only ones who have become accustomed to taking all the liberties they deem necessary with UN resolutions.
>
> (Borradori 2003: 111)

In the confluence of all universals and singularities that is the moment of 'now', this is not even remotely realizable for Derrida. That the strategy can be one of working towards an imaginable future through the very ambiguities and discontinuities of the imaginable as such, is the hope for the future we cannot anticipate. We cannot anticipate that future from the place and time of our 'now', since for it to be absolutely the future, it must also be absolutely other in its own monstrous futurity. Any future we can now imagine cannot, by definition, be a future at all in this sense, merely the repetition of the 'now' and the insistence that it de-institute even the possibility of a future in the absolute otherness of future's difference to now. It is also an insistence, then, that the 'now' of now continues to replicate itself as the certainty of its knowledge of itself as such.

The issue of ethics

In the context of this chapter the issue of ethics emerges as an issue not of what ethics is or is not, but rather of *thinking* ethics and the possibilities open to cultural criticism on the bases of thinking ethics differently. In this sense, the issue of ethics *for* cultural criticism becomes an issue of the ways in which different possibilities for thinking ethics can be made to circulate. Ethics in these terms is not something that cultural criticism can be said either to have or not to have. Rather, it may point to the questions which arise within its own paradigms and procedures. Quite how those questions may be addressed will remain open to debate, but to answer them, especially definitively, is no longer a disinterested possibility, even in the masquerade of its being so.

If ethics, understood in this way, can no longer reside in splendid isolation, then one of the issues it entails and also traces as such, is that of the 'other'. What constitutes the 'other' conceptually and procedurally, becomes a matter of struggle on the site of that other. If we are, in Derrida's terms, to act ethically towards the other in the singularity of its otherness, then two further questions come to the fore: (1) what can be thought in the name of the 'other'; and (2) how may we approach it in terms of that thinking?

The magnitude of such questions is not to be underestimated, and they manifest themselves as an issue in critical and cultural theory today in the field of alterity.

4 Alterity

- Why alterity?
- The dialectic of self and other
- Cultural difference
- Infinity and exhalation
- The issue of alterity

Why alterity?

In the preceding chapter, the possibilities of ethics were explored in relation to the concept of the 'other' and to the operation of that other within the self-same. While the other was sketched there, the chapter itself pointed to the need to explore the concept in greater detail. This exploration is, of course, the work of this chapter, but it is performed here under the sign of **alterity**. Alterity, while signifying other or otherness, also carries the trace of a series of theoretical developments which set out to de-institute the fetish of the other and, at the same time, to continue to explore the possibilities opened up to cultural criticism by thinking of the other as a relationship both of difference and deferral.[1] Here, the significance of the other as a concept, becomes that of attending to the function of otherness as both inside and outside of that to which it is other. The issue for cultural criticism, marked by the sign alterity, is one in which the problem of accounting for cultural difference can operate in relation to the terms of both the universals and particulars of difference itself. This will involve the development of theoretical models already in circulation within this book, as well as an examination of what is at stake in different ways of approaching the other as a set of cultural possibilities. Inevitably, there is a continuity here with the work on ethics begun in the preceding chapter, and this will be foregrounded in the final section of this chapter by exploring the consequences of an understanding of the other for what some critical theorists have analysed as ethics. This is inevitable since, as issues, alterity and ethics also overlap, weaving the territory of both as they are submitted to analysis. What emerges, however, is a broader understanding of both.

That alterity is an issue in cultural criticism is evident in its growing concern with an attention to cultural difference. From the 'problems' of refugees and asylum, through notions of home and hospitality, to those of multiculturalism and hybridized communities, the issue of alterity haunts cultural analyses in the twenty-first century. Together with race riots across Europe, bombs in public spaces, and the concentration of the otherness of the other in the siege mentality of 'them' and 'us' in the wake of '9/11', the question of the other persists in cultural analysis. What is clear from the different possibilities unleashed by all the concepts and events just described is that frameworks for thinking alterity matter – not just to the reified environment of the academy, but to the function of cultural criticism in its relation to the world.

The dialectic of self and other

As early as 1976, Jean Baudrillard (1929 –) argued that the twin towers of the World Trade Center, in New York City, stood as a sign in architectural form for the capitalist monopoly that is now America's dream of itself. In themselves, he wrote, the twin towers are a perfect monopoly in that their doubling 'signifies the end of all competition, the end of every original reference' (1993: 69). In a doubling of his own, perhaps citing himself as a gesture within the end of every original reference, Baudrillard was later able to rework this analysis into what became a 'Requiem for the Twin Towers' in the wake of their destruction in 2001:

> Perfect parallelepipeds, standing over 1,300 feet tall, on a square base. Perfectly balanced, blind communicating vessels (they say terrorism is 'blind', but the towers were blind too – monoliths no longer opening on to the outside world, but subject to artificial conditioning). The fact that there were two of them signifies the end of any original reference. If there had been only one, monopoly would not have been perfectly embodied. Only the doubling of the sign truly puts an end to what it designates.
>
> (Baudrillard 2002: 43)

In the doubling of the sign, Baudrillard argues any originality of the referent is lost and we accede to simulation. But there's also a sense in Baudrillard's argument that the doubling marks the uncertain possibility of the referent in the first place. In this reading, the monopoly of power symbolized in the twinning of the towers as though it were absolute is also the mark of its anxious vulnerability. That those towers became the object of destruction is, therefore, no surprise to Baudrillard since they simultaneously signify what he terms an 'arrogant power' of violent global monopolization and at the same time instigate a resistance to that power in the very sign they establish:[2]

> There is, admittedly, in this cloning and perfect symmetry an aesthetic quality, a kind of perfect crime against form, a tautology of form which can give rise, in a violent reaction, to the temptation to break that symmetry, to restore an asymmetry, and hence a singularity.
>
> (Baudrillard 2002: 46)

Unnervingly, but perhaps explicably in Baudrillard's terms, the destruction of the symbolic symmetry of the towers was also enacted in the form of a duality: 'a double attack, separated by a few minutes interval, with a sense of suspense between the two impacts' (2002: 46). Here the doubling foregrounded by the towers is also the source of its destruction, leading Baudrillard to question whether the collapse of the towers was, symbolically, an effect of destruction (from without) or implosion (from within). As physical objects, the towers were destroyed by the impact of the planes, but as symbolic object, they imploded:

> The collapse of the towers is the major symbolic event. Imagine they had not collapsed, or only one had collapsed: the effect would not have been the same at all. The fragility of global power would not have been so strikingly proven. The towers, which were the emblem of that power, still embody it in their dramatic end, which resembles a suicide. Seeing them collapse themselves, as if by implosion, one had the impression that they were committing suicide in response to the suicide of the suicide planes.
>
> (Baudrillard 2002: 47)

Here, the doubling gesture of the towers is in turn doubled by the violence of its destruction, and results in a further doubling in destruction. As both inside the object as a result of the impossible contradiction there, and outside the object as an effect of the response it invokes to the symbolism it struggles to embody:

> The symbolic collapse came about, then, by a kind of unpredictable complicity – as though the entire system, by its internal fragility, joined in the game of its own liquidation, and hence joined in the game of terrorism. Very logically, and inexorably, the increase in the power of power heightens the will to destroy it.
>
> (Baudrillard 2002: 49)

Doubling, twinning, cloning, are all signs not only of iteration but also, and perhaps always, of an anxiety about the referent in iteration. In Baudrillard's model, that anxiety haunts the iteration of the symbol and finally destroys it.

In the instance of the twin towers, what they signify is possible through the relation between the two and the interval in time and space between the two terms of that relation. Both as architectural form and as symbol, the towers struggle to establish mastery as a final realizable point. In this sense, the doubling is also uncanny in that it points to the impossibility of a certain point of origin reminding, in this case the world, that it is never at one with or to itself. If the singularity of the one tower can be supplemented by the second, there's no reason conceptually to stop at two. The logic of the supplement is that what it supplements is always already lacking and therefore infinitely supplementable.

Perhaps the uncanny effect of the doubling, represented by the towers in Baudrillard's analysis, is not limited to the reminder of lack for which the supplement serves, but can also be traced in the very necessity of difference in the circulation of signs through which cultures constitute themselves. In this sense, the doubling can be understood as the repetition of the same, but also as the attempt to annihilate difference in a gesture of indifference towards it. Here, the monopoly of the same is not only a violent gesture towards the other, but also the destruction of the same in its desire to finally expunge the other from its ontological horizon and rid itself of its dependence. While the other indeed serves to remind us that we are not all there is, any attempt to erase that other by making it the same is ultimately self-destructive.

One account of the radical dependency of the same and other is, of course, that found in theories of signification explored in Chapter 1. And, it is clearly theories of signification that Baudrillard draws on in his analyses of 'symbolic exchange'. Another account of the radically uncertain dependence of same and other, is given by psychoanalysis in its task of thinking through what makes humans subjects of culture, and the consequences that can be said to arise from the process of that making.

In the film *Single White Female* (Schroeder 1992), another kind of doubling is explored, this time in terms of the relation of human self to other and the consequences of that relation for subject identity. Disillusioned with her boyfriend, who no longer reflects or is worthy of her love, the lead female Alison Jones seeks out a 'perfect' room mate and appears to find her in the character of Hedra. As the film unfolds, however, Hedra's presence becomes increasingly unsettling both *to* Alison and *for* the audience. Hedra begins to take on Alison's life for herself, first by appearing the same as Alison – cutting her hair in the same way, adopting her mannerisms, wearing her clothes, and so on – and then by replacing Alison in Alison's own life – by becoming the perfect object for the ex-boyfriend and standing in the place of Alison in the world. Finally, it emerges that Hedra has been a twin who lost her sister at an early age and, was compulsively seeking to make up for that loss by redoubling herself in her relation to Alison. Hedra has, of course, lost her grip on reality, but the consequence of her insistent doubling is that it destroys the self–other relation by erasing the difference on which it is founded. As Baudrillard suggests in relation to the twin towers, 'the doubling of the sign puts an end to what it designates' (2002: 43). Not only is the self–other relation disintegrated by the erasure of difference here, but the component parts of that relation are also destroyed. The film, perhaps inevitably, recuperates the anxiety it instigates and all is well, at least for Alison, by the end. Hedra's psychosis, however, proves to be her downfall and, for the sake of Alison and implicitly the audience, she is suitably punished for her annihilating gesture towards the other.

In psychoanalytic accounts of subject formation, however, the 'blame' of psychosis is not so easily made, and the anxiety of the subject not quite so easily recuperated. As we observed in Chapter 3, for Jacques Lacan, the subject emerges as an effect of the confluence of the three dependent orders of the imaginary, symbolic and real. Within that confluence, the subject is also held in a dialectical relation to the other as the little 'o' of other people and/or objects within which the subject may appear to find itself. This relation is dialectical since it works both ways – it is mutually constitutive of what appear to be its two parts. Without that possibility of recognition, the subject cannot maintain its sense of self in the imago of the Ideal I. In his account of the treatment of psychosis in the *Écrits*, Lacan goes back to Freud for a model of this interdependent relation in what was Freud's Schema L (Figure 4.1):

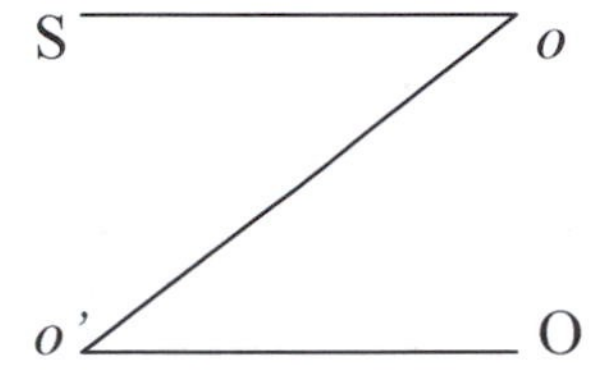

Figure 4.1 Schema L

> This schema signifies that the condition of the subject S (neurosis or psychosis) is dependent on what is being unfolded in the Other O. What is being unfolded there is articulated like a discourse (the unconscious is the discourse of the Other), whose syntax Freud first sought to define for those bits that come to us in certain privileged moments, in dreams, in slips of the tongue or pen, in flashes of wit.
>
> (Lacan 2003: 214)

Here, the condition of neurosis or psychosis depends on what is being unfolded in the Other (O). It is not, in other words, self-contained within the subject fixed in the S of the schema, but relationally dependent in a movement through two further forms of little '*o*' on its way to the big 'O' that the symbolic represents. Further, what is unfolded there is *like* a discourse – the discourse of the Other – in the sense that it narrates the possibilities for the subject as subject in its terms. But, if the discourse of the Other were entirely outside the subject, why would they be interested in it? For Lacan, the subject is 'interested' in the discourse of the Other since it is in part founded there, but also in the sense that the sign 'interest' carries of investment in material terms:[3]

> Why would the subject be interested in this discourse, if he [*sic*] were not taking part in it? He is, indeed, a participator, in that he is stretched over the four corners of the schema: namely, S, his ineffable, stupid existence, *o*, his objects, *o'*, his ego, that is, that which is reflected of his form in his objects, and O, the locus from which the question of his existence may be presented to him.
>
> (Lacan 2003: 214)

The subject participates in the discourse of the Other in the *interest* of self as self-recognition, and it is in this participation that the subject is able to reflect on its own existence as such. As such, however, the subject is stretched over the four corners of the schema. In a sense, the four corners then become the co-ordinates of the subject's possibilities in its relation to the other and the Other, Understood in this way, the possibilities of the subject's undoing are also revealed in the contingency of the process and something of the terror of that undoing may emerge.

Although the schema is used here to analyze the condition of psychosis, it also designates the condition of subjectivity itself. Here the subject (S) depends on a relation to the Other (O) and what is unfolded there. However, there are detours on the trajectory between S and O, which account for the constitution of subjectivity in its particularities. The first detour is through *o*, which for Lacan represents the subject's objects. That is, all the objects significant to the subject in reflecting something of his or her imagined form of existence. This detour takes the subject through the space of the ego (*o'*) – that which is reflected of (his) form in (his) objects – which is, in turn, formulated or held in its fantasy through the objects. The trajectory then arrives at the place of the Other (O) as the realm of the symbolic, wherein the subject is granted representation in the form of a position within language, as well as from the other (*o*) in terms of the due recognition garnered from the other in the subject's sense of itself in its idealized form.

The subject maintains a version of the imago, then, but only at the behest of the other in its capacity to recognize the imago projected on to it and to allow the subject to recognize that recognition in a place outside of the subject. When we ask 'Who am I?' for Lacan we ask it of the other and the Other. What we find there is never an answer in itself – in the other – but rather the possibility of a further question 'Where am I *there*?' [my emphasis]

(2003: 214). This further question returns, in the movement of the schema, to what was apparently its point of origin – the subject who asks the question. But that subject is no longer original or authentic even to itself since it is now only 'that' which it can appear to find 'there'. For Lacan, this is a model both of the ongoing process of the subject's realization of itself as such, and of the process by which neurosis or psychosis, as dislocations in the relation to the symbolic, may be redirected in the course of the psychoanalytic process.[4]

In Lacan's model, difference is not only foundational of the subject, but also a vital aspect of its maintaining a meaningful sense of itself in the world. When Travis Bickle asks of his own reflection 'What you lookin' at?' in the film *Taxi Driver* (Scorsese 1976), we know he has lost it not only because he is talking to himself, but also because the self-referentiality of the gaze implies that he can no longer function as a *social* subject from the place of his entrapment in the narcissism of self-sufficiency. But, of course, this too is an illusion. Travis' terms of reference may be problematic in that they seem to be entirely his own, but even there they are stretched across co-ordinates which effect estrangement. He no longer recognizes himself in the symbolic image and he perceives the other he sees in his place there, as a threat. The final gesture of annihilation of that other is also symbolically the annihilation of any form of rational self Travis can have.

In an attempt to avoid the possibility of suggesting that films simply show us real life, we may perhaps recast the significance of the analogy *Taxi Driver* provides in terms of what it can represent *there, for us*. The pleasure of the text can in part be derived from the fascination of the disintegration of a subject that is *not us*. But, this already implies at least a second part and, that is the fascination with the horror of the monstrous other – out there in the world of other people – whose desire to annihilate is realized for us in the serial murder of the proxy. Both are recuperable thrills within the terms of the film as film, since they are not actually happening to us. There is a mastering distance in the relation of dominant specularity afforded the viewer, between the film as film and the reasoned place of knowledge the subject is granted by the film in that relation.[5] In the possible identification with the anti-hero, however, the film foregrounds a further possible pleasure/displeasure which is not so easily closed off. That is, the condition of dependence of the subject on the other and the estrangement *within* both to which it gives rise. In one sense of it, this is the further possibility that plays across the genre of horror as a whole. What Marlowe, for example, remarks on as horror in Joseph Conrad's novel *Heart of Darkness* is not simply the indeterminate horror of finding Kurtz, having 'gone native' in the jungles of the African Congo, finally capable only of uttering 'The horror! The horror!' (1994: 100). It is also the horror of the worst possible encounter between Europe and its other there: 'Well, you know, that was the worst of it – this suspicion of their not being inhuman' (1994: 51).

While Schema L is, as Lacan points out, a simplified sketch of the continual process of subject formation, affirmation and reformation, it may serve to develop the metaphor of the mirror stage of development elaborated in Chapter 3. For Lacan, as we have seen, a notion of self comes about *in* the Other as the symbolic order – but also *from* the other – as an effect of the dialectical relation between self and other, in which self is recognized in its own particular idealized form. To remind ourselves briefly here, passing through the mirror stage, the human acquires a notion of self in the form of an identification both with the other and with the symbolic order which promises to represent it in the metaphor of the mirror's reflection. For Lacan, this is fundamentally a *misrecognition* since the identification made can never, by definition, be identical with the other. What the infant learns at the mirror stage, therefore, is to recognize a differentiation between itself and the world – including the world of other people – which surrounds it. However, in the process of separation described there, the infant is also opened up to desire as the desire to be *for* the other. That is, to be recognized by the other not only as worthy of recognition, but also as the ego-Ideal imagined at the moment of identification.[6] Since this ego-Ideal, and the necessity of recognition in its terms from the place of the other, occur for Lacan in the order of the imaginary, the notion of self acquired at the mirror stage is necessarily doubly precarious. It is at once both a misrecognition and one which is enthralled to the other. In this moment of its constitution, then, the possibility of the subject – its dialectical relation to the other – is also the possibility of its undoing.

We need the other to define ourselves, but we need a particular other who will grant us recognition in the terms we demand. Writing about the impossibility of love in *The Four Fundamental Concepts of Psycho-Analysis*, (1991) Lacan suggests that love is a state of fantasy, of deception, since love involves seeing another seeing you as you would like to be seen. This may be an ideal, but as a reciprocal relation it can never be fulfilled except temporarily in the imaginary, since it radically depends upon the other and the other's willingness to acknowledge that recognition in the return of the gaze. There is always the possibility that the dialectic of recognition will not be accomplished, and Lacan suggests that this is the moment at which love breaks down, or implodes. Here love reveals the aggression towards the other necessarily already entailed within it: 'You never look at me from the place from which I see you' (1991: 103). Within this formulation, difference is foundational. The subject comes to be the subject by virtue of a fantasy of recognition from the Other both in terms of its position within the symbolic but also spectrally in the gaze of the other.

But if the infant is directed towards the other in this sense, it is also eventually constituted in a further relation to language. For Lacan, the infant takes this initial separation, of difference, from the mirror stage into the symbolic and into the identity it will then acquire within forms of representation. At the most basic level, the promise of representation is made available to the subject in its taking up the position of the 'I' within language, although since language is itself a system of differences for Lacan, this second identification is also a misrecognition. In addition, since the 'I' of language is merely a signifier, it is entirely indifferent to the subject that appears to recognize itself there, marking as it does a position rather than an identity. Implicitly, of course, if 'I' marks a position, then in any identification with 'I', I make an identification with a position not my own but belonging rather to the logic of the system that that language is. There is a very real sense, Lacan concludes, contrary to our assumption of mastery there, that 'language speaks us'. By taking up the position of the 'I' of language, by identifying myself with it, my self is identified by it in particular terms which not only are not controlled or defined by me but also, of course, pre-exist me. In this sense, the subject's entry into language marks the socialization of human being, but while it offers the possibility of meaning, it is only ever within its terms.

For Lacan, then, the subject is represented by the signifier in the order of the Other as the order of the symbolic. But the signifier is by definition exterior and thus oblivious to the subject constituted there. While we may be motivated to take up the borrowed and shared position of the 'I' of language in order to make representation of ourselves to an other, even the Other, language prohibits the possibility it promises. The signifier, as Lacan points out, 'is that which represents the subject for another signifier' (2003: 350). It does not, therefore, represent the subject for another subject. Our desire – perhaps to represent ourselves to the other – is thus impossible, since in language we are simply strung temporally along the chain of signification. Desire, then, becomes 'the desire of the Other' in at least two senses. Desire is *for* the other – to be constituted in the present and masterful position we misrecognize in the imago that emerges as an effect of the mirror stage – and desire is *from* the other – in the will to be recognized by the other as we would wish to be recognized, having misrecognized an ego-Ideal. Writing in *Écrits*, Lacan thus states that in establishing the notion of:

> the Other with a capital O as being the locus of the deployment of speech (the other scene . . . of which Freud speaks in *The Interpretation of Dreams*); it must be posited that, produced as it is by an animal at the mercy of language, man's desire is the desire of the Other.
>
> (Lacan 2003: 292)

A great deal, then, can go wrong for the subject. Foundational yet precarious, the relation of the subject to the other in difference is located in desire as the motivation to be whole – not lacking the possibility of being in meaning and so not enthralled to the other. But given the subject's foundation in that originary lack, desire also becomes the desire to be for the other and to master the threat to the ego-Ideal of the subject acquired from that relation. It is in this sense, for Lacan in *The Four Fundamental Concepts*, that what love is also always entails aggression. The fantasy of self depends upon it. What Lacan terms the movement of desire is thus the movement that motivates, and perhaps regulates, the behaviour of the subject in any social situation. Understood as movement, desire informs the subject's perceptions and actions, and at the same time keeps that subject within the movement of desire. In this sense, the subject is constituted in a kind of perpetual motion constantly seeking imagined fulfilment from *petit objet a*, and defending its ego-Ideal from whatever may prevent its achievement there. While it may temporarily appear to have arrested that movement, in what Lacan terms the '**points de capiton**' (2003: 170), these prove merely to be anchoring points and thus temporary moments of respite in the endless movement of desire that being a subject in meaning necessarily entails.

The possibility of failure for the subject – of failure of recognition from the place of the other as the ego-Ideal – is for Lacan an absolute possibility. That is to say that it is a fundamental condition of being a subject, and so is an effect of a relational necessity rather than the particularities of a given social situation. Difference is thereby constitutive of subjectivity. While difference is an absolute in this sense, however, this does not mean that it is therefore not open to, even implicated in, the particularities of different social relations. On the contrary, the dialectical relation of self to other manifests the potential for aggression on both sides of the dependent relation at every possible turn. What forms such aggression may take, the ways in which the preservation of the imaginary Ideal may manifest itself, are precisely determined by the subject's being in the world of culture, of value and of differing relations of power.

Cultural difference

If difference is foundational, as Lacan asserts, then the estrangement and subsequent anxiety to which it gives rise will manifest in subjects as they operate in 'socially elaborated situations'. This pertains to everything from the foundation of nation-states to the policies and procedures which nation-states operate in relation to what, in their foundation as such, becomes their 'other'. One arena within which the issue of the socially elaborated other is focused for cultural criticism today is that of the stranger, the foreigner, the other within.

Race riots across Europe and bombings in public spaces, as well as mass protests by 'illegal workers' who are not citizens in the USA, or of Aboriginal claims to 'land rights' across Australia, attest to the issue of the other in the everyday of contemporary cultural politics. Indeed, the 'list' is continually supplemented – by 'ethnic cleansing' in the Balkan states of Europe and in a number of African countries, as well as in Iraq and Turkey, even to some extent in the history of relations between India and what is now, since partition, Pakistan.[7] Often violent action is taken and lives are lost daily. Clearly, as an issue, difference matters within the world. But, if difference is foundational, then are some differences more real or more important than others? For anyone engaged in cultural struggles over meaning, there will of course always be instances within which the priority of one particular manifestation of difference will seem more urgent than another. But the particularities of difference are, potentially at least, endless. If it is to approach the question of difference, in its particularities in cultural difference, in more than simply relative terms, then cultural criticism must have some ground upon which to operate that does not essentialize difference, and does not fix it in relation to a truth which can be multiplied by competing claims of different differences. Founded on a notion of truth, however we conceive of that truth, difference would ironically be no more than subservient to it.

One discussion, which has gained prominence in the wake of the race riots in France and the bombings on the London transport network in 2005, has focused on the possibilities for the relationship between self and other in different forms of social organization. Models, for responding to difference through assimilation or multiculturalism, provide a focus for addressing the questions of managing the specificities of cultural difference in particular social situations.

As a model, assimilation prioritizes the dominance of self in relation to the other by conceptualizing the nation as guardian of the interests of the people – *all* people, as *one* – and thereby conceiving of the stranger as that which can be accommodated by becoming the same as the community it joins. Founded on the principles of 'Liberté, égalité, fraternité', the modern nation-state of the French Republic responds to the presence of the other within by insisting on assimilation to its terms. Muslims, for example, must become French by relinquishing markers of difference – the enforcement of the ban on wearing the hijab in school being the most notorious recent example. In order to be French, citizens of France must all be French in the same way.

Britain, on the other hand, operates towards a model of multiculturalism within which there must be a core of sameness – what it means to be British – to which difference may be added and so respected for what it is in its own terms. Here, conceptually at least, diversity becomes a marker of Britishness so long as the core values of belonging in Britain are upheld. Amusingly, the British government is currently working on what it calls the 'British Citizenship Test', which includes a certain proficiency in the English language, knowledge of key historical facts, an understanding of 'the role of women', and loyalty to the crown and the parliament.[8] While debate continues over what 'key' is, what historical facts are, and what the 'proper' role for women in Britain might be, I'm still not so sure I'd pass.

While Britain and France, in part, also constitute themselves in relationships of difference to one another which are often competitive, the social models each operates also become sites of another sort of struggle for dominance. The high moral ground is said to rest differently within each. As models, however, neither has worked to achieve the ends it imagined. Petrol bombs on the streets of Paris attest to wide-ranging perceptions of exclusion, marginalization and discrimination against self-identified groups of people within mainstream French society. Similarly, the bombings in London in 2005, carried out by four men who had until that moment seemed to be happily different citizens of Britain, attested to a violent sense that the interests of citizens in Britain were not as one.

Debate, which will continue as a condition of France and Britain's establishment of themselves, now rages on how to approach the other in order to defuse the other. Of course, all such debate, no matter what its hue, is resolutely taking place from the position of an assumed self-same.

However, the question for cultural criticism remains that of how it might read such socially elaborated situations. One possible avenue of thinking on this terrain is that opened up by the French Marxist, Louis Althusser (1918–90). Having enthusiastically worked for the classic Marxist notion of the material conditions for revolution, Althusser was one among many intellectuals to be disillusioned by the events of 'May '68'.[9] Faced with the question of why, when the material conditions appeared to be right, the people did not seize power, Althusser was forced to rethink his model of ideology in relation to its operation in and through the concept of the subject.

For Althusser, ideology seemed to work more intimately at the level of the subject, by a process of 'hailing' he described as 'interpellation' (Easthope and McGowan 2004: 47). In this model, subjects are surreptitiously interpellated into cultural positions within which they are invited to recognize, and so identify, themselves. One crucial aspect of this model of interpellation, is that no subject is simply called to recognize itself in terms of a singular position. As subjects, we are hailed continually by different calls to recognition and identification, some of which may well be contradictory. I may, for example, find a sense of myself within my identification in a profession and at the same time within my identification with 'the people' on the council estate where I grew up. Being a subject, then, is being a subject 'there' in ideology, but not monolithically so since ideological positions are never singular or *fixed* in the subject for all time. Subject to competing ideological forces, the subject becomes the site of a series of possible ideological contradictions. While each force affords the subject a sense of self within its terms, it can never do so entirely or for all time.

Two consequences arise from Althusser's proposition about ideology as a hailing process: the first is that the subject is over-determined and thus the site of multiplicities which are constantly in negotiation and hence movement; the second, which inheres in the first, is that the subject is motivated to seek ways out of the contradictions which comprise it and so affect the possibility of change. Change is motivated in Althusser's model by the discomfort of the subject in the spaces where ideologies overlap, spaces which he terms 'the interstices' (Easthope and McGowan 2004: 48). While subjects may seek to change the conditions of their subjectivity, however, for Althusser, they can only do so within, and so as an effect of ideology. There is, in other words, no position outside of ideology.[10]

While some cultural criticism has manifested itself in a form of arresting the play of contradiction which Althusser's work points out – for example, Spivak's 'strategic essentialism' discussed in Chapter 3 – it does so in terms of a position implicitly outside of the terms and conditions of knowledge which produce it as necessary in the first place. For the British cultural critic Stuart Hall (1932–), such a move is not only inadequate, it is also counter-productive in that it merely replicates the structures of value it seeks to disrupt. Writing on the signification of 'black', in 'black popular culture', for example, Hall urges a theoretical move which does not rely simply on affirming the difference of cultural difference:

> The essentializing moment is weak because it naturalizes and dehistoricizes difference ... The moment the signifier 'black' is torn from its historical, cultural and political embedding and lodged in a biologically constituted racial category, we valorize, by inversion, the very ground of racism we are trying to deconstruct.
>
> (Hall 1992: 30)

Another avenue of thinking difference, which is also dependent on the first, is that opened up in the work of Homi K. Bhabha (1949–) in the concept of 'hybridity'.[11] For Bhabha, hybridity seems to offer the way out of conceptions of the social subject as either one or the other of the cultural difference signalled in the relation self–other. Taking Althusser's notion of the interstitial aspects of subjection as the place of the ambivalence of subjectivity, Bhabha argues that the ambivalence of hybridized identities, in what has become a global community, now serves as the 'proper' grounding of a cultural politics of difference. Here, difference gives way to instances in which it is called into question. For Bhabha, it is in the interstices, the spaces in between incompatible identifications that the subject may henceforth experience or, be constituted by, ambivalence. Ambivalence has a special function here in that it opens what is most obvious and apparently true about the subject to question, doubt and, above all, the possibility of denaturalization. Bhabha's concept of ambivalence, then, plays in the margins of the text, and the subject *as* text, in the form of a *movement*. That is, an 'interstitial passage between fixed identifications opens up the possibility of a cultural hybridity that entertains difference without an assumed or imposed hierarchy' (1995: 4). Here the ambivalence of identity as hybridized, even within itself, gives rise to a different kind of movement for Bhabha – the movement between two places as a movement of delay, pause and interval, within which doubt about the logic of the relay between two 'things-in-themselves' can play.

In some ways, this begins to sound very much like Derrida's approach to what we may term the play of the 'a' in differance. Where Derrida argues that there can be no universal to differance, however, for Bhabha, hybridity and the ambivalence generated there become principles of action with specific, culturally determined, goals. For Derrida:

> Differance does not *resist* appropriation, it does not impose an exterior limit upon it. Differance began by *broaching* alienation and it ends by leaving re-appropriation *breached*. Until death. Death is the movement of differance to the extent that that movement is necessarily finite. This means that differance makes the opposition of presence and absence possible. Without the possibility of differance, the desire of presence as such would not find its breathing space. That means by the same token that this desire carries in itself the destiny of its non-satisfaction. Differance produces what it forbids, makes possible the very thing it makes impossible.
>
> (Derrida 1973: 143)

If differance is not an opposition, then it is not grounded by anything outside of itself, such as presence. It is nothing more or less than play, a movement in both space and time, and as such it is never either present or absent. To think of it in the service of something outside of itself is to annul differance (with an a) in the name of difference (without an a) and so to arrest its potential for disruption. Differance, in Derrida's terms, calls the very possibility of any and all assertions of presence or absence, inside or outside, radically into question.

Ironically, if meaning arises as an effect of difference, which is one sense of it implied in Bhabha's formulation of hybridity, then difference gives rise to *all* meanings. For the specific argument made about race by Bhabha, the logic of the proposition of difference does away with the particularities of difference as stable points of comprehension. Since it generates everything, it becomes a new universal. Further, the notion of 'interstitial relations' presumes, as the second part of the sentence makes clear, fixed identities as a form of presence, and one which is in turn originary. In other words, hybridity and its attendant operation of ambivalence, as Bhabha defines it, rely on a notion that in *the first place* identity is fixed and singular, but is made by culture and society into something multiple and potentially contradictory. While this privileges difference(s) in identifications, it removes the radical potential of difference as a founding effect of the subject from *within* the very condition of subjectivity itself. That is, difference as there in *the first place* rather than acquired as a supplement later on in cultural life. Difference in hybridity, however transformative it may be understood to be, therefore becomes something external to the subject, and an addition to its originary unity.

This is doubly problematic. In the first place, the argument in relation to hybridity is paradoxical. As Pnina Werbner has pointed out in writing about the 'dialectics of cultural hybridity':

> The current fascination with cultural hybridity masks an elusive paradox. Hybridity is celebrated as powerfully interruptive and yet theorized as commonplace and pervasive ... The paradox leads us to ask about the cultural *limits* of cultural hybridity, demarcated not only by hegemonic social formations but by ordinary people.
>
> (Werbner 1998: 1–2)

The 'limits' of cultural hybridity may well be marked by what Lacan suggests is its displacement of difference from inside – the subject estranged from itself as a very condition of subjectivity – to the outside – of culture, society and discrimination. Difference located outside implies that the subject, untainted by 'bad' cultural forces, would be harmonious both to itself and in relation to others. Without culture as such, the subject would therefore be human, and so at ease. While it would be foolish to suggest, even for a moment, that Freud and Lacan were 'right' about the subject and Bhabha was somehow 'wrong', it's difficult to comprehend how any notion that the organic human outside of culture is not entirely selfish, aggressive and demanding – given as it is, in the psychoanalytic model, at least by instincts and drives in its originary animalistic existence. Yet, the further limits of hybridity exceed even this account. Like strategic essentialism, there is certainly a case to be made here that the concept of hybridity reinstates a universal which remains universal regardless of its multiplicity. As 'powerfully interruptive' and yet 'commonplace and pervasive' in Bhabha's terms, difference is everything and so in a sense, nothing. As everything, it marks something like truth in its universality. As nothing, it loses its force in relation to the very thing it seeks to assert – particularity.

So, assimilation, multiculturalism, hybridity, even ambivalence, do not realize the possibilities of harmonious, or just, relations of cultural difference that they are mobilized to serve. One way of understanding this failure might be to think of it in relation to Lacan's proposition that there is no 'Other of the Other' and that anywhere such an Other is posited, it is by definition an imposter. What this implies for cultural criticism is that there cannot be a position within it which it is not called to account for itself with precision. There is no position, to continue Lacan's analogy, from which the truth of the Other may be glimpsed. As was suggested in Chapter 3, the model which psychoanalysis proffers on the terrain of cultural difference – *all* and *any* forms of cultural difference – is one in which the desire for and to master the other is always inherent to the condition of being a subject in the world. Here, the ethics of psychoanalysis is the ethics of accepting and facing that condition, rather than denying it. This leads to a notion of perpetual and unrelenting critique, even in relation to models of critical thinking which seem in certain circumstances to be the right way to proceed.

For Derrida, in relation to his own critical practice, the operation of perpetual critique is crucial. In dialogue with the psychoanalyst Elisabeth Roudinesco, Derrida comments that:

> a general ethic of vigilance seems necessary with regard to all the signals that, here or there, in language, in advertising, in political life, teaching, the writing of texts, etc., might encourage, for example, phallocentric, ethnocentric or racist violence.
>
> (Derrida 2004b: 28)

This does not, and should not for Derrida, rule out the possibility of finding an assertion of presence even in the critiques of presence which he himself offers. While vigilance is crucial, it is also still necessary to count within the reach of vigilance the pretext of being vigilant itself. In the dialogue that takes place in the name of 'Of the anti-Semitism to come', Derrida elaborates on the harsh impossibilities of his own accounts:

> It is true that the very form of my question remains imprudent. It seems to assume that, although 'before us,' and however close to us it may be, even here among 'us,' anti-Semitism remains external or foreign to you and me, to others as well. I'm afraid that no one can claim immunity here. For my part, I always try, perhaps with mixed success, to watch myself very carefully when it comes to the authorization I sometimes risk giving myself – as a Jew or as someone identified as such, and therefore supposedly as someone who cannot be suspected of anti-Semitism – whenever I ask critical or sometimes radically 'deconstructive' questions about Judaism (religion or culture), Jewishness, the notion of election, about a certain communitarian dimension, or about the foundation of the state of Israel, especially, or its politics for the last half a century.
>
> (Derrida 2004b: 110)

For Derrida, this involves a particular kind of play as a form of question which does not simply arise from external relations but also the internal relation of estrangement within the subject. While common sense necessarily 'forgets' this estrangement, or banishes it from the subject to the place of the 'abnormal' subject, cultural criticism must move beyond the territory delineated by such sense-making processes. Difference, for Derrida, must be alert to difference at every instance of its manifestation:

> Nothing matters for me as much as my Jewishness, which, however, in so many ways, matters so little in my life. I know very well that such statements seem contradictory, lacking in common sense. But they would be so only in the eyes of someone who could say 'I' only in one whole piece, only by expelling from himself [*sic*] all alterity, all heterogeneity, all division, indeed all altercation, all 'explication' or 'coming to terms' with oneself. I am not *alone* with myself, no more than anyone else is – I am not *all-one*. An 'I' is not an indivisible atom.
>
> (Derrida 2004b: 112)

This is a powerful call for cultural criticism. It carefully avoids the difficulties encountered in concepts of strategic essentialism, hybridity and ambivalence, and it calls for cultural criticism perpetually to account for itself in the terms of the vigilance of self-critique. If 'I' am not an indivisible atom, then I am never an innocent fixed point of perception, no matter where I fantasize 'myself' to 'be'.

Infinity and exhalation

As long as the relation between self and other is founded on difference or estrangement within the subject which cannot either be reconciled or overcome, then that relation will always entail the appropriation of the other for the self in love and/or aggression as the defence of self in the face of the other. For Derrida, while this may produce a useful understanding of the way things are, it does not necessarily work to forge a different kind of future – especially one which it is difficult, if not impossible, to imagine today. In his work on ethics, Derrida turns to the work of the French and German philosophers, Emmanuel Lévinas (1905–95) and Edmund Husserl (1859–1938) in an attempt to point towards a different set of possibilities yet to come.

Writing in *Totality and Infinity* in 1961, Lévinas proposes a model for thinking the self–other relation which Derrida revisits in his own essay 'Violence and Metaphysics' in 1967. For Lévinas, philosophy, and in particular phenomenology and ontology, has proceeded from an implicit totality of knowledge.[12] Within this, the other is reduced to an object of consciousness for philosophy in that it is grasped, approached or thought of in terms of the network of the philosophy within which it is thereby simply placed. Thus, the approach that philosophy makes to the other is always within the violence of the metaphysics which always already comprehends that other within the terms of the same. In other words, philosophy seeks to grasp the other and in so doing reduces what Lévinas calls the 'absolute alterity' of the other to the self-same. In particular, Lévinas sees this operation in the work of Husserl in his *Cartesian Meditations* which constitutes the other in terms of the self-same as an alter-ego. For Lévinas, however, unless and until this priority of the self, which he terms egoic, is disrupted, any hope of an ethical approach to the other is lost. To move beyond the egoic, we must move to the limits of phenomenology, and it is these limits that Lévinas seeks to explore. Understood in the absoluteness of its alterity, the other has the capacity to transcend the metaphysics of reason by which anyone comes to be able to think that they 'know' in the first place.

The key to this for Lévinas is in challenging the self-assurance of the subject who thinks that they know. As long as we understand and can grasp the objects out there in the material world, then that world remains entirely and only within the terms of our idea of it, and as such does nothing to disturb or to challenge that idea. In this sense, philosophy forestalls any exposure of its own limits from any unanticipatable place which, in not being anticipatable, may exceed it. The potentiality for realizing those limits exists, for Lévinas, in difference understood as absolute other to what we think we know. If we approach the other as absolutely other in a radical alterity from 'us', then what Lévinas calls a 'face-to-face encounter' may take place, and within this a relation of exchange can occur. If the other is not already constituted in our expectation of it, then the glance which is reciprocated in the intersubjective exchange becomes one of question rather than answer. The other is not 'there' for us in the sense of a surety of presence, but rather in an absence understood as what we do not yet know will come from the place of the other. The glance, from the subject to the other and from the other to the subject, then becomes one of interrogation, of interlocution and of exchange, which has the capacity to shift the metaphysical consciousness of each:

> Absolute experience is not disclosure; to disclose, on the basis of a subjective horizon, is already to miss the noumenon. The interlocutor alone is the term of pure experience, where the Other enters into relation while *καΘ'ύτb* where he [*sic*] expresses himself without our having to disclose him from a 'point of view,' in a borrowed light. The 'objectivity' sought by knowledge that is fully knowledge is realized beyond the objectivity of the object. What presents itself as independent of every subjective movement is the interlocutor,

> whose *way* consists in starting from himself, foreign and yet presenting himself to me.
>
> (Lévinas 2003: 67)

The object of knowledge, then, must remain a noumenon or thing-in-itself, as Kant had envisaged it.

If 'I' am to remain open to the possibilities of the other, not as a version of me but leaving his or her otherness intact as such, then 'I' must be divested of the ego of consciousness as I know it. While this may seem to hint towards the sacrifice of self to the other, for Lévinas, this cannot be the case since such sacrifice would annul the subject and make the other a totality akin to that of a theological God. Exchange and revision on both sides of the difference, marked by the subject's encounter with the other, must be maintained if its radical potentiality is to remain open. For Lévinas, the questioning glance of the other 'calls' the subject to account to the other and so to attempt a meaningful response. What results is something like a dialogue between two absolutely different logics of meaning making, from which in turn an interrogation of the limits of each may take place.

While this can only be affected in language, in the exchange as question, the arbitrary nature of the values that appear obvious in each language become exposed. I must answer the call from the other to explain myself to the other (and s/he to me). Of course, I can only do that in the terms of the metaphysics I inhabit and, as we observed in Chapter 1, that metaphysics will be replete with the arbitrary assumptions and cultural values generated there, as well as the arbitrary system for generation that metaphysics is. While these are arbitrary assumptions, values and systems that remain entirely other to the corresponding metaphysics that constitute the other, they will be exposed as such to me (and to the other) in the questioning glance of the exchange between the two. By opening 'my world' to the other, I open that world to the question of the other. I become, in other words, aware of the arbitrariness of my own systems of meaning making and at the same time, so long as I remain open to the other in its absolute alterity, I may glimpse a responsibility for those arbitrarinesses towards the other. It is in this sense that ethics for Lévinas becomes possible.

Introducing a further distinction in language, between what he terms 'the saying' and 'the said', Lévinas details the possibility of an exchange between subject and other which, while questioning and unsettling, also leaves open the possibility of the autonomy of each. Here the said remains at a distance, an interval, from the saying, such that anything said may be opened to question without necessarily annulling the possibility of further actions of saying. The dialogue thus proceeds.

Totality, of thought and system, remains total for Lévinas only as long as the unpredictable spontaneity of the exchange is forbidden. Once it is not, once the ban of my ideas or of my existence as the only possible ideas or existence is lifted, then what becomes possible is potentially limitless. As Lévinas writes:

> Without substituting eschatology for philosophy, without philosophically 'demonstrating' eschatological 'truths,' we can proceed from the experience of totality back to a situation where totality breaks up, a situation that conditions the totality itself. Such a situation is the gleam of exteriority or of transcendence in the face of the Other. The rigorously developed concept of this transcendence is expressed by the term infinity.
>
> (Lévinas 2003: 24–5)

Devoid of any religious faith in an ultimate truth (eschatology), a different kind of faith becomes possible for Lévinas. This is a faith in what cannot be known from the place of the self-same, not to replace it but to transcend it. It is in this open possibility – the unpredictability of the transformation – that is ultimately, for Lévinas, where the ethical may operate. Infinity here is, importantly, not totality replaced by a radically unstructured chaos. Opened to the permanent critique from the place of the other, totality is exposed as essentially incomplete and thus implodes within its own logic. In that implosion, however, opened to another way of knowing, totality can be transcended. And it is this sense of transcendence that Lévinas posits as the infinity of his title. Infinity is not the opposite of totality in this sense, but the trace of the possibility of moving beyond its limits.

However, that faith, even devoid of its eschatological frame, is nonetheless based on a certainty which is left unexamined in Lévinas' schema. For Derrida, that certainty is the certainty both of the subject as complete to itself in its illusion of self, and in the priority of consciousness in the concept of the subject as all there is.

In his own reading of Lévinas' proposition of the potentiality of infinity, as he describes it in *Totality and Infinity*, Derrida both notes and seeks to critique the possibilities opened up by Lévinas' work. In the first instance, Lévinas' account of philosophy depends on a rejection of that philosophy as inadequate to the task of thinking ethically if ethics is to mean thinking the other as absolute alterity. For alterity to be thought in its absoluteness it must be outside of philosophy as that which is absolutely other to it. What Derrida points out in 'Violence and metaphysics' (2004a) is that while Lévinas is right to suggest that metaphysics performs a kind of violence on the other by appropriating it into the same and/or else violently expunging it from its terms, what he proposes retains its own dependence on the metaphysics he claims to transcend. Metaphysics, however impartial, is for Derrida all we have and, after all, it is also what produces the very possibility of the concept of the other in the first place. In this sense, the infinity of the absoluteness of the other is not strictly outside of the totality it seeks to displace.

In the second place, Derrida contests Lévinas' contention that the absolute alterity of the other is maintainable as an outside to something which, implicitly at least, remains inside as something which is initially given. There is no account of the subject in Lévinas which is not estranged from and to itself within its subjectivity. There is no uncertainty, in other words, prior to the encounter with the other. In this sense, the subject of metaphysics is presumed to be a perfect subject present to itself in the illusion of presence that metaphysics grants.

For Derrida, these observations suggest the need for two further developments of Lévinas' model. The first suggests a return to the scene of Lévinas' model of the possibilities within a phenomenology, such as Husserl's, which are simply discounted. The second suggests a further insistence on the possibilities that may arise from within a model of the subject as other to itself, prior to entering the exchange with the other in Lévinas' metaphor of the face-to-face encounter. While for Husserl, the face-to-face encounter is conceivable by recourse to a primordial state of being which comes before meaning, for Derrida, this is not an answer to Lévinas since it still maintains the notion of an outside, or another place, from which a greater truth may be drawn. However, the pressures of a real which may be traced in being in meaning, not as a primordial remainder but rather as a trace which keeps meaning from itself within the subject, do not necessarily have to be discounted. For Derrida, there is no need to decide between being as organic form independent of consciousness, and consciousness as independent of something which is not consciousness.

In a gesture of vigilance, in which he reminds us of the importance of in *For What Tomorrow* quoted above, Derrida begins the task of exploring the possibilities of an ethical relation to or with the other, which is both de-pendent upon but also critical of the assumptions left unchallenged in Lévinas' delineation of the ethics that arise from absolute alterity. We 'live in difference' Derrida concludes at the end of 'Violence and metaphysics', on neither one side nor the other of the oppositions that structure both us and the world in our idea of it. While there is no Other to the Other of metaphysics as the possibility of subjects' consciousness, there might still be a 'real' which continues to operate beyond our idea of it. What that is cannot, by definition, be thought, but that does not mean that we can, necessarily, dismiss it.

In *The Gift of Death* (1996), Derrida turns from Lévinas' notion of a conscious approach towards the other as conscious to itself, towards a notion of exhalation which is not necessarily conscious of itself as such. While exhalation presumes an exhaler, it is not one which is determined necessarily merely by consciousness. Breathing is something that humans do autonomically. We don't have to think about breathing in order for breathing to happen, and while 'brain death' might prohibit breathing, it is not alone in the capacity it holds in that direction. The failure of vital bodily organs, for example, independent of our thought of them, can affect the same possibility. In this sense, exhalation marks for Derrida the material immateriality of the subject not as either consciousness or organic being, but rather an effect of both. In this way exhalation marks a form of radical ambivalence. This can have no remainder, since there is no inside nor outside to it, and therefore no interval between what might constitute the self and other. Exhalation, as a kind of breathing, marks the place from which it emanates as itself a place of question. Both empty and nonetheless possible, breath empties its capacity for presence in the presentation of itself as exhalation.

The issue of alterity

Is alterity best thought of as an inevitable foundation *within* subjectivity giving rise to aggression, which must always be acknowledged as such even in the masquerade of benevolence? Is it best thought of from the place of the other through the experience of the other as enhancing the experience of self? Or, should experience, wherever it is posited, be called to account for the illusion of a completeness to itself inherent in it from the very start?

Lévinas' notion of the radically other as a mark of the limits of consciousness of self, in a reciprocal encounter, may not attend to the innate otherness within the subject and the ensuing inevitability of aggression as posited by Lacan, but it does seem to offer something on the question of how the other – as the stranger or foreigner – may be approached in ways which do not simply perform the violent act of appropriation. It is perhaps clear from the approaches of nation-states to the actions of those deemed foreign to them – either because they literally come from a place and so a metaphysics which is different, or because they inhabit a different set of values within the same place that demarcates the nation – that the anticipation of the other in his or her otherness deflects the possibility of equal exchange. What seems evident, is that the totality of a dominant metaphysics is always presumed as if it were the only possible way of both conceiving of the world and ways of being within it. A model in which the other marks the limits of metaphysics and can prompt attention to those limits in a capacity for transformation on both sides of the subject–other relation is certainly attractive in these terms. Both would, however, have to be equally open and committed to the process of engagement. They would also, as Lacan and Derrida both remind us in different ways, have to be divested of the very terms that make the subject possible in the first place. As such, any encounter could only take place between subjects divested of the terms and conditions of being in meaning that subjectivity marks.

Perhaps there is no rush to decide between the two. As an issue, alterity can remain open and in a sense, as with the issue of ethics before it, resist any attempts to resolve it, describe it, and to annul it by pronouncing finally upon it. Perhaps alterity should continue to function, in *all* aspects, as a question in cultural criticism, rather than the place of an answer. If it is to do this, however, then the function of alterity will be that of marking the limits of cultural criticism. As a question rather than an answer, alterity would neither be within nor without cultural criticism. It would not be a definite presence of something else which could then be quantified and evaluated, but rather a kind of spectre which in its haunting continually reminds us that what we know is not all there is.

As such, the issue of alterity both overlaps with that of ethics and at the same time points to another of the issues within critical and cultural theory which is both contested and fundamental, that is, the question of the real. How cultural criticism thinks about the question of the real, how it constitutes it and circulates that constitution within its terms, becomes crucial and must, as a result, also be made available to a corresponding scrutiny of its terms and possibilities.

5 The Real

- Why the real?
- The real as simulation
- The real as void
- The real as real
- The issue of the real

Why the real?

Notoriously, the Wachowski brothers' film trilogy *The Matrix* (1999, 2003), poses a series of questions about the real which seem to encapsulate contemporary suspicions about it. What is it, how do we know it, and is it really 'out there'? The answers, however, are clear from the start: the real is outside of the matrix, Morpheus knows this because he has passed down the rabbit hole, in sense, to some virtual place beyond the matrix and yes, it is really out there, although mere mortals are kept from it by the net of reality the matrix casts. Neo too can transcend the matrix if he picks the right pill and opens his mind to the possibilities of thinking beyond the laws that the symbolic of his world parades in front of the real in order to hide it. Disappointingly, the world outside of the matrix resembles every other dystopian vision of the world in ruin. It is a nasty place that no one would want to inhabit. However, within the real, Neo discovers supra-human powers which depend not on his physical being but rather the capacity of his mind. Indeed, what the real world teaches Neo is that mind freed from the shackles of the matrix really can determine being. Neo can leap impossible lengths, but only if he knows he can. If he thinks, Neo can be free. But, as Morpheus points out, it is not sufficient for Neo to believe, he must *know*. He cannot have faith in something outside of himself, Neo must know and know fully within and to himself. He must be sure of the power of his own mind.

Billed as an interrogation of the real, *The Matrix* has surprisingly little to say that might not already have been anticipated by Marx in the principle of false consciousness.[1] However, it does focus some of what is at issue with the concept of the real within critical and cultural theory and the cultural criticism that is produced there. Whether it is configured as a simulation, purely an effect of signification, as a void resisted in the imaginary and covered by the symbolic, or as real in the sense of being out there but unknowable, the real persists as a question for cultural criticism. How the real is thought, and the possibilities to which different modes of thinking it gives rise, will therefore be explored in the course of this chapter.

The real as simulation

The claim that *The Matrix* somehow encapsulates a sense that there's something not quite right with the real as we perceive it is an interesting one and in this sense justifies the foregrounding of Baudrillard's *Simulations* in the first film. In his work on simulation, Baudrillard outlines a theory of simulacra as a third order of assumed relations between representation and the real. In the first, representation is presumed merely to stand in for the real, to reflect it or embody it, and so to have a direct relation of correspondence. A bone of Christ bought by a pilgrim may in the terms of this order stand directly for the thing it is understood to represent. In the second order, the proximity of the relation is stretched. With the advent of technologies of mass production and reproduction, the immediacy of the real original representation is lost and value becomes redirected towards the perfectibility of the reproduction. In this sense, we may prefer a poster of the *Mona Lisa* to the real original of the painting, since its colours are ironically more authentic, uncontaminated as it is by the vagaries of 500 years, and you don't have to fight with everyone else at the Louvre to catch a distant, and so less complete or accurate, glimpse of a disappointingly small original trapped behind bullet-proof glass. In this order, something like Warhol's *Marilyn* series also affirms a different kind of value, for the reproduction. While these paintings/prints/ photographs affirm their value, as a new kind of original, they also call into question the very notion of the original by foregrounding the structured nature of the real from which they are derived.[2] In this case it is relatively easy to read the original photograph of Marilyn Monroe for all of its techniques for producing the image irrespective of any reality of the person of Marilyn herself. While the copy differs from the real in this order – it is now a copy of a copy – there is still a sense that the copy relates to an original even if that relation is distanced from it. The third order, the order of simulacra, however, breaks with any notion that there is a connection direct or otherwise between the real and representation. Here, in the saturation of the image in global media technologies, representation loses sight of the real and circulates as though it has no need of any point of reference beyond itself in order to guarantee the value of its signification. In this order, the copy is the copy of the copy for which no real original can be said to exist.

While Baudrillard allows that the orders of signification may have some involvement with historical time and conditions of production, however, he is also careful to resist situating simulation in any order of a real. For

Baudrillard, the relation between the real and representation has always been imaginary rather than real. As such, it is possible that for one pilgrim who clutched the bone of Christ in reverence, there was at least another who did not. Equally, in the postmodern world of virtual realty it is still perfectly possible to cling to a notion that the real can be manifest directly in representation – that the *Mona Lisa* really is an accurate and, therefore, valuable reflection of a real woman we'd love to 'know' as da Vinci did, or that '9/11' survival narratives tell the truth about what really happened and must, therefore, be enshrined as such.

If the relation between representation and the real has always been an imaginary one for Baudrillard, however, this is not the same as claiming that there is no real or that the real is imaginary. On the contrary, the real is woven like a thread through Baudrillard's work, providing an often unstable aspect of different analyses of social attitudes towards it. Avoiding a negative theology, in which a statement, such as 'the real is dead', merely confirms the absolute certainty of the referent of the real, Baudrillard's discussion becomes one of questioning, within which the 'problem' of the real continues as problematic. Neither a conceptual thing, nor the absence of such a thing, the real in Baudrillard's work becomes a form of resistant non-compliance within any cultural certainty that it has been mastered:

> 'Why is there nothing rather than something?' There is, ultimately, no answer to this, since the nothing originates in myth, in the original crime, whereas something originates in what, by convention, we call reality. Now, the real is never sure.
>
> (Baudrillard 1996: 13)

The 'crime' to which Baudrillard refers here, is the 'perfect crime' of the murder of the real to which he adds, in his Introduction to the book *The Perfect Crime*, 'the crime is never perfect'. The consequences of the crime, however, are 'never-ending' and the real is 'never sure' since it is not simply reduced to the either/or of nothing or something.

The real persists for Baudrillard even when we believe we have done away with it, since belief itself is imaginary. The real remains intangibly real, however, and therefore marks the limits of consciousness as both imaginary and symbolic. Consciousness does not touch the world since it is both produced and limited by the rules of symbolic exchange and as such, refers only to itself. That we may have faith in human thinking, believing in its capacity to rule the world in our idea of it, the real reminds us of the futility of such thinking. As Baudrillard writes: 'Our consciousness, by which we aspire to outdo the world, is merely a secondary excess, the phantom extremity of a world for which this simulation of consciousness is entirely superfluous' (1996: 10). Simulation here equates to consciousness as determined symbolically and, as such, that which is entirely self-referential. What we think we know is produced and maintained within what we produce as knowable and the world in our image of it is thus, an effect of simulation. It produces the thing it appears simply to find. In this way, simulation has nothing to do with the real of the world, merely our idea of it. While it may appear that global technologies have committed the perfect crime of the murder of the real, that crime itself remains imaginary since, if it is a murder at all, it is one which is enacted on and in simulation itself. The real continues along its way, and reports of its death are greatly exaggerated.

However, the persistence of human belief in its own mastery through consciousness envisaged as total, does produce effects. Ice caps do melt, genes do mutate, and death comes to us all in spite of any mastery we may imagine we have in its direction. For Baudrillard, the 'will' that humans have both towards the world, and towards a belief in the world as *envisaged*, is potentially disastrous. The real, he argues, is not real since in our comprehension of it as such, it becomes other to itself in human consciousness:

> So no purpose is served by attempting to reconcile the order of will with that of the world to the philosophical advantage of the latter. There is the continuity of the world as, in secret, it is nothing and means nothing. This latter does not, strictly speaking, exist. It cannot be verified, but can only betray itself, only 'show through' [*transparaître*] like evil, squint out through appearances. There is no dialectic between the two orders. Each is alien to the other.
>
> (Baudrillard 1996: 15)

The two orders have no dialectical relation. There is no real relation between the real and representations of it, merely the notion of a relation produced in the futile desire for mastery within the symbolic.

While the two orders are alien to one another in this way, however, there is something of the order of the real which 'shows through'. For Baudrillard, no matter how perfectly symbolic mastery appears to reign, the human is haunted by the perpetual ghost of his/her own mortality. While a great deal of human knowledge is directed towards mastering the finality of human being, the real will persist in 'showing through'. At best, humans succeed only in erecting symbolic obstacles for warding off the finitude of existence. Virtual reality within which your virtual self may die and rise again, cloning techniques within which perpetual existence of the self-same may be imagined, even the structures of inheritance in a capitalist economy are all, for Baudrillard, techniques designed to ward off mortality. What they demonstrate, however, and perhaps ironically, is the insistence of mortality and the direction of human will towards an overcoming which, were it ever to be achieved, would succeed only in erasing the human from its own phenomenal existence. The *perfect* crime, Baudrillard suggests:

> is that of an unconditional realization of the world by the actualization of all data, the transformation of all our acts and all events into pure information: in short, the final solution, the resolution of the world ahead of time by the cloning of reality and the extermination of the real by its double.
>
> (Baudrillard 1996: 25)

This is certainly not to insist that the real either exists or does not exist conceptually for humans. Indeed, perhaps the very will to the perfection of the crime attests to its lack and that the subsequent rush towards the decision, to know and so to transcend the uncertainties of the real as neither/nor, is counter-productive. For Baudrillard, what he calls the 'value of thought' does not rest in its convergence with 'truth' but rather its 'immeasurable divergences which separate it from truth' (1996: 94):

> The point is not, then, to assert that the real does or does not exist – a ludicrous proposition which well expresses what that reality means to us: a tautological hallucination ('the real exists, I have met it'). There is merely a movement of the exacerbation of reality towards paroxysm, where it involutes of its own accord and implodes leaving no trace, not even the sign of its end. For the body of the real was never recovered. In the shroud of the virtual, the corpse of the real is forever unfindable.
>
> (Baudrillard 1996: 46)

What we think we find is, by virtue of the finding, always already simulation since simulation produces the effect of the possibility of the finding in the first place. What simulation finds is always what it is possible to find within its own terms. And, for Baudrillard at least, this has nothing to do with any *real* real except that generated within self-referential terms. We may continue to ignore the pressure of the real as unknowable within signification, but we do so at a cost. Interestingly, that cost is not the cost borne by a real world, in the sense of a direct exchange – your totalities of consciousness hurt the environment – but rather a cost understood in terms of dissent. While the latter can, of course, include the former, it is not delineated by it. The real as question persists for Baudrillard in the possibility of its constant circulation and thereby, its potential to keep the process of the question alive.

Within the broader project of his work, Baudrillard posits the role of cultural criticism as that of the work of terrorism. We must not consent, he argues, to the rule of reason but rather work to 'obfuscate' within what reason believes it knows. The 'absolute rule,' he asserts: 'is to give back more than you were given. Never less, always more. The absolute rule of thought is to give back the world as it was given to us – unintelligible. And, if possible, to render it a little more unintelligible' (1996: 105). In this way, the project of cultural criticism is the project of persistent denaturalization of its own terms of reference. This becomes a further persistent 'showing' of its limits.[3]

For another critical thinker, however, the project, when it comes to the real, is a very different one. Indeed, for the Slovenian writer Slavoj Žižek (1949–) the real is and must be intelligible. For Žižek, cultural criticism must work to tear the veil of signification from the real in order to expose it for what it is: nothing.

Drawing a distinction between the 'early' and 'later' writings of Lacan, and favouring the 'early', Žižek rejects the notion that the real *is*. That is, he refuses the possibility of the real as something-in-itself which is beyond the differential grasp of symbolic systems even while it continues to exert a kind of pressure there. The real, for Žižek, is a void. In this sense, what is there for Žižek as a relation to the symbolic is nothing as a paradoxical form of troubling presence which the symbolic serves to mask or to make up for. This is significant to Žižek since it continues to produce an effect in the subject in the imaginary. In the place of the real as nothing, Žižek argues, the subject erects a fantasy – an object, a figure, a fear – in order to shield itself from the abyss of nothingness that it cannot bear to confront.

The real as void

In this schema the subject is founded on the basis of lack, as it is in Lacan. However, for Žižek, the foundational absence of the subject comes not from the movement from organic being into the realm of meaning, which cannot comprehend it, but rather as an effect of the symbolic itself. The subject is lacking in this sense since it is constituted in a system which cannot support it, a system that is with no positive terms. In a chapter on Hegel and language in *For They Know Not What They Do* (1991), for example, Žižek writes that the symbolic works by a logic of internal negation:

> Exception: what we can never obtain is a complete set of signifiers without exception, since the very gesture of completion entails exclusion.
>
> Therein consists the fundamental paradox of the 'logic of the signifier': from a non-all, non-universal collection, we constitute a Totality not by adding something to it but on the contrary by subtracting something from it, namely the excessive 'besides' the exclusion of which opens up the totality of 'all things possible'.
>
> (Žižek 1991: 111)

Signification, then, is paradoxical of its own accord. From nothing but difference, the symbolic itself creates the totality of everything possible by excluding contradiction – the work of the exception, the excessive 'besides' – which might reveal the impossibility of the totality thereby created. In this way, everything is created in signification from nothing by the negation of the negation.[4] Something appears from the site of nothing in the dialectical process of redoubling. Just as, linguistically, the double-negative produces a positive – 'I ain't got nothing' produces in effect its opposite 'I have got something' – so the negation of negation, for Žižek, produces the semblance of a something as an effect only of itself.

In this sense, the negative real becomes the absent centre of the symbolic, an absence which 'hollows out' the symbolic and thus excludes from it what Žižek calls the 'hard kernel of the real', a radical nothingness at the heart of every something.

Since the real is a negative in Žižek's terms, the symbolic cannot operate in relation to it and, as a consequence, the symbolic has what Žižek terms 'no external support' (1991: 112). It is not, therefore, that the real delimits signification, but rather that its constitution as the absent centre of signification makes signification itself a logical impossibility. The 'problem' for the signifier, Žižek writes:

> is not its impossibility to touch the real, but its impossibility to 'attain itself' – what the signifier lacks is not the extra-linguistic object but the Signifier itself, a non-barred, non-hindered One. Or, to put it in Hegelese: the signifier does not simply miss the object, it always-already 'goes wrong' *in relation to itself*, and the object inscribes itself in the blank opened up by this failure. The very positivity of the object is nothing but a positivization, an incarnation of the bar which prevents the signifier from fully becoming itself.
>
> (Žižek 1991: 112)

The real does not simply precede the symbolic then, but appears after the fact in the negative space opened up by its own failure. While for Lacan, the real marks a limit to signification – as the systematic possibility of what is – for Žižek, the real comes about as an effect of the failure of signification to attain nothing but itself. In this sense, the real is paradoxically real only in its nothingness, which in turn has nothing to do with any real as such, except as an effect in and of the symbolic.

If the real is an effect of the symbolic for Žižek, then the subject too is an effect of language and, as such, emerges on the borderline of the paradoxical absence as presence of signification, agonistically strung between the impossibility of presence and the possibility of absence. As a consequence, as Žižek neatly puts it: 'The subject is an empty place correlative to antagonism:

social fantasy as the elementary mode to mask that antagonism' (2005: 282). The subject is correlative to antagonism since it is constituted in language, which as a system is nothing, and in the movement only towards its own annihilation: death. To feel oneself as nothing moving only towards death is, of course, intolerable. Somehow the cheap cliché 'life's shit and then you die' doesn't really seem to cover it. What *does* cover it, however, or at least for Žižek, is fantasy as ideology. With the subject so precariously placed, ideology moves convincingly through fantasy to secure the subject, at least, a *sense* of a place in the world.

In this sense, in the absence of the real as something, ideology works to protect the subject by helping to maintain the fantasmatic screen between itself and the nothingness upon which its concept of self irredeemably rests. Culture, and specifically cultural objects, in this sense ward off the possibility of psychosis in which fantasy collapses in on itself for lack of an external prop. In other words, the superfluous spoils of a capitalist economy are enough to keep the subject bound to that economy since they secure for us all a fundamental sense of ourselves.

Leaning on Lacan as he does, this fantasy is not for Žižek the simple false consciousness of Marx, but rather a complex social dialectic always enacted in relation to the other. Just as Lacan's mirror stage suggested the enthralment of the ego to the duality of the desire to be for and to master the other, so the concept of the dialectic of the subject advanced by Žižek further displaces the possibility of the subject to the in-between of subjects, in the plural social space. This he calls the 'inter-dit' or the inter-subject spoken by the symbolic as difference.[5] Here, my sense of myself is gained at the expense of the other in a dialectical relation with an other – not me – and the agonism/antagonism engendered within the subject on the basis of its own foundational lack, is projected outwards onto other social subjects who are thus, made to act as 'scapegoats' for my own worst fears.

In Žižek's work, this is most convincingly demonstrated in analyses of the social antagonism of racism or inter-ethnic conflict founded on cultural difference.[6] Here, not only is racism an effect of the desperate need of the subject to expunge the antagonism of its own foundation in difference, it is also an effect of the subsequently precarious dialectic of opposing fantasies in which the other itself designates the possibility of one's own undoing. In these terms, the answer to the question 'Che vuoi?', what does the other want from me, is both 'to demonstrate that it is where I cannot be' and 'to take from me the place where I can be'. In either case, the other represents only a threat to *my* fantasy.

Writing of what he calls 'the figure of the Jew' as the figure of collective social hate in Nazi Germany, for example, Žižek points out its dual function as fantasy. In the first place, it apparently realizes the fantasy that the other is here to take what must belong to me, and in the second, simultaneously, it ensures the maintenance of the fantasy of the 'me' harmoniously there to be robbed in the first place. Neither fantasy is, of course, real. Both mask the absence of the real. In this sense, the figure of the Jew in a particular context at a particular time, functions as the mythical scapegoat of destruction which threatens an otherwise, yet equally fantastic, sense of stable organic community:

> What appears as the hindrance to society's full identity with itself is actually its positive condition: by transposing onto the Jew the role of the foreign body which introduces in the social organism disintegration and antagonism, the fantasy-image of society qua consistent, harmonious whole is rendered possible.
>
> (Žižek 2001: 90)

Just as it is with signification for Žižek, the negative – in this case, the figure of the Jew as hindrance to society – is retrospectively made positive in the negation that if it were not for the Jew, all would be well. While the figure of the Jew has nothing whatever to do with the real, its negative constitution has the counter-intuitive effect of positively maintaining the equally fantastical sense of community, by exclusion from it.

As an analysis of racism, this is plausible since it deconstructs the ground of the real on which racism as such legitimates itself. Racism is, therefore, a fantasy structure, albeit one which has dire material consequences, and so has no foundation in anything uncontestable, such as the real. In this way, ideology harnesses a notion of the otherness of the racial other to the foundational operation of the social subject in its maintenance of itself. And, as a result, it would seem to work efficiently. The inevitable question, however, is how we engage and contest this efficiency.

Surprisingly, for Žižek, there is only one answer. In order to loosen the grasp by which ideology fixes us, we must go through the fantasy to the void it masks. And, if this sounds painful, then that's essentially, or rather psychically, because it is. Indeed, throughout his writing Žižek again and again returns to the concept of trauma as the site of the possibility for what he designates as 'traversing the fantasy' [la traversée du fantasme] to the place of the real. Trauma marks a traversal of fantasy for Žižek, in that it is constituted in the subject's encounter with the horror of the real as nothing – an encounter which implies the subject's own impossibility. 'All we have to do,' Žižek writes, 'is to mark repeatedly the trauma as such, in its very "impossibility", in its non-integrated horror, by means of some "empty symbolic gesture"':

> This, then, is the point where the Left must not 'give way': it must preserve the traces of all historical traumas, dreams and catastrophes, which the ruling ideology of the 'End of History' would prefer to

> obliterate – it must become itself their living monument, so that as long as the Left is here, these traumas will remain marked. Such an attitude, far from confirming the Left within a nostalgic infatuation with the past, is the only possibility for attaining a distance on the present, a distance which will enable us to discern signs of the New.
> (Žižek 1991: 273)

Here, trauma marks the possibility for the subject of glimpsing that which we had mistaken as the real in the fantasy which masked its absence, was always already nothing more than an illusion. By traversing the fantasy we enact a refusal to comply with the ideology which associates itself to it, creating a 'degree zero' from which it is then possible to recreate the fantasy again but perhaps differently.

In the final section of *The Ticklish Subject*, Žižek goes on to define the terror of the real as nothing in terms of 'good' and 'bad' and what he posits as the 'authentic act' – of the subject – as an 'inherently terroristic' forced choice (2000: 377). In these terms, the choice is then two: good *or* bad. But, how we decide which is which is far from straightforward.

Since the real is the absence on which signification is founded, reality is merely the game of fantasy in relation to signification. As such, the force of the authentic act of the subject lies in its capacity to redefine the rules of that game. The ethics of this, however, rest on a basis of self-annihilation since the act is enacted by the subject that is also nothing but an effect of the game. If the force of the act redefines reality, then that necessarily includes what Žižek terms 'the very basic self-identity of its perpetrator' (2000: 377). A 'proper' political act, he continues, 'unleashes the force of the negativity that shatters the very foundation of our being' (2000: 377). Using the accusation often levelled at Stalinism, that it was ultimately terroristic, Žižek insists that the Left is not to be discouraged from seeking more stringently the 'good terror' over the 'bad'. We must learn, then, to distinguish or to *choose* between the good and the bad of terror because terror is all we have.

In his analysis of '9/11', Žižek invokes once again the distinction drawn in *The Ticklish Subject* between good and bad terror as 'authentic-' and 'pseudo-' acts (2000: 378). Within these terms, the destruction wrought that day designates not an authentic-act, but rather a pseudo-act since, while enacted, it is, nonetheless, fully within the fantasy rather than traversing it.

In part, this is because, as many cultural commentators have subsequently noted, the World Trade Center explosions were events conducted in 'real time' on TV screens across the globe. In this sense they were, while having a material effect, nonetheless perceived in virtual reality. For Žižek, virtual reality is not real but rather the fantastical simulation which masks the absence of the real. It is, he remarks in *Welcome to the Desert of the Real*, like a decaffeinated coffee: 'offering the product deprived of its substance: it provides reality itself deprived of its substance, of the hard resistant kernel of the Real ... experienced as reality without actually being so' (2002: 11). In other words, the pseudo-event, or act, is the ultimate fantasy since it masks the absence of the real with the empty simulation of the real in a kind of double bluff. Enacted on TV screens over and over and over again, the image of the real stood in for the real as a copy of something for which the concept of an original could no longer be sustained. It became for Žižek, a 'special effect' which outstripped all other subsequently pale Hollywood imitations in its apparently being offered as more real than real. As such, all that '9/11' could represent for Žižek was yet more evidence of the sameness of the apparently 'new' of the 'new' millennium:[7] 'The authentic 20th Century passion for penetrating the Real Thing (ultimately, the destructive void) through the cobweb of semblances which constitutes our reality thus culminates in the thrill of the real as the ultimate "effect"', (2002: 12). Not only did the televised 'realtime replays' avoid the real by the semblance of showing it, but the real as void was deftly obliterated by the possibility of glimpsing the unthinkable as a form of repackaged consumer product.

Thus, the inauthentic act merely recirculates the fantasy in the name of a real which cannot be realized because it is nothing. In doing so, it creates the desire for the impossible encounter with that real which it is readily able to fulfil. The real is thus not beyond signification, but once again fully within it. For an act to be authentic in the 'postmodern cult of scepticism' which Žižek delineates as the cultural moment of our now, any notion of the real as untouchable must be abandoned. This, he argues, is the only possible 'ethics of the real':

> we should abandon the standard metaphorics of the Real as the terrifying Thing that is impossible to confront face to face, as the ultimate Real concealed beneath the layers of imaginary and/or symbolic veils: the very idea that beneath the deceptive appearances, there lies hidden some ultimate Real Thing too horrible for us to look at directly is the ultimate appearance – this Real Thing is a fantasmatic spectre whose presence guarantees the consistency of our symbolic edifice, thus enabling us to avoid confronting its constitutive inconsistency ('antagonism').
>
> (Žižek 2002: 31–2)

This notion of an 'ethics of the real' is again elaborated in *Interrogating the Real*, where Žižek argues that what is masked by the fantasy is the truth that there is none. Again, this belongs not to something that cannot be comprehended, but rather to the symbolic field itself:

> the fact that the signifying field is always structured around a certain fundamental deadlock. Thus, deadlock doesn't entail any kind of

> resignation – or, if there is a resignation, it is a paradox of *enthusiastic resignation*: we are using here the term 'enthusiasm' in its strict Kantian meaning, as indicating an experience of the object through the very failure of its adequate representation. Enthusiasm and resignation are not then two opposed moments: it is 'resignation' itself, i.e. the experience of a certain impossibility, which incites enthusiasm.
>
> (Žižek 2005:282–3)

There are, it would seem, a number of issues raised by this formulation of the 'act' and of 'traversing the fantasy', not the least of which might well be the paradoxical concept of the subject as sufficiently present to itself – in spite of the fantasy that marks the impossibility of that – to choose to act beyond the fantasy that constitutes it. If traversing the fantasy means penetrating and so de-instituting the myth that enables the subject to sustain the illusion of being, then how, or by what, is the fantasy traversed?

It's not just that the being of the subject would be disillusioned, but that in the process of disillusioning it would recede into the abyss of nothing. In which case, without being, how can I act? There has to be an 'I' there, sufficiently present to itself in the first place, in order to enact the de-realization. In order to step outside of the fantasy, I have paradoxically to be immune to the fantasy, in which case, why step beyond it? Back onto the stage of the symbolic and the real, then, there comes the **Cartesian** Ideal of the subject which, in its exercise of mind, may determine its being. This is no secret in Žižek, but rather one of the explicit aims of his work from the outset. The spectre haunting European discourse is, he argues in *The Ticklish Subject*, 'the spectre of the Cartesian subject' and the project of the book as a whole is to 'reassert the Cartesian subject whose rejection forms the silent pact of all the struggling parties of today's academia' (2000: 3–4). One of those parties would be Lacan, at least the Lacan of 'The subversion of the subject and the dialectic of desire' (2003) for whom the Cartesian Cogito is no more than a form of idealism.

Lacan traced back through the antecedents of Hegel and Kant, is a Lacan, some have argued, read against itself.[8] That aside, the Lacan of Žižek takes cultural criticism along a very different trajectory to that advanced by Lacan in his own critique of what he saw as the 'immanentism' fundamental to Hegel (2003: 333). Indeed, in 'The subversion of the subject and the dialectic of desire', Lacan explicitly argues for a notion of the real which does not depend on *any* idea of it.

The real as real

Can the real be neither juridical nor liberatory, neither void nor excess, but still somehow 'there', beyond comprehension? The answer, for both Lacan and Lyotard is not simply that it can, but more urgently that it must. It must if critical thinking is to continue to resist and contest the totality of meaning as it appears to us as subjects of it.

For Lyotard, we discount the real – either as merely an effect of the symbolic or the imaginary – at our peril. Addressing the prediction of the explosion, or death, of the sun in 4.5 billion years time, Lyotard points out that without the sun, no animal or plant life is possible: 'With the disappearance of earth, thought will have stopped – leaving that disappearance absolutely unthought-of of. It's the horizon itself that will be abolished and, with its disappearance, your transcendence in immanence as well' (1993: 9–10). No matter how diligently subjects work to imagine that life is sustainable in the absence of the sun, or to prove symbolically that the sun exists only in our idea of it and is therefore somehow irrelevant to our existence, if and when the sun ceases to be, humans will not continue to live. No matter how sovereign we believe ourselves to be, we will be obliterated. Of course, science, as a set of knowledges, may be wrong about the death of the sun, even as it is set at such a distance from our 'now'. But that does not change what would be the effects on life of the sun's disappearance.

While the death of the sun may seem an extreme and distant possibility, death itself is not. One indisputable condition of being human is mortality. No matter how convincingly I imagine that death will not happen to me, it will. And no matter how complexly I seek to understand it conceptually or to relegate it merely to the order of signification as an illusory effect, it will happen. Death is real then in the sense that it exists independently of my consciousness of it, that it defies attempts at interrogation, and that it marks an ambivalent limit to what I can know. I can conceive of what it might be like to die, and I can talk about it, but I cannot and will not ever experience my own death. If 'I' am there to do the experiencing, then 'death' is not. And, of course, if 'I' am not there, I cannot either imagine or symbolize it. Death exerts a pressure, however. While it may never be fully within my imaginary and symbolic grasp, it does, nonetheless, produce a structuring effect. My life consists in some ways of anticipating it, either by repression or expectation. I will be wrong about both, but that does not mean that I am not, in some sense, traversed by it.

For Lyotard, the indisputable real as ambivalently neither fully inside the subject nor outside of the subject but nonetheless real, is crucial. In part, it is crucial since any account of the human, albeit cultural, which discards the real also paradoxically discards the human. But it is also crucial to philosophy as a model of critical thinking since for Lyotard it radically alters the trajectory of philosophy's own accounts of thinking itself:

> You explain: it's impossible to think an end, pure and simple, of anything at all, since the end's a limit and to think it you have to be on both sides of that limit. So what's finished or finite has to be

> perpetuated in our thought if it's to be thought of as finished.
> (Lyotard 1993: 9)

So long as matter is 'X'd out' of philosophical thinking, thinking has nothing to contribute to life or to the future possibilities of thinking the being of being human, and for Lyotard this is, as he puts it, 'the sole serious question to face humanity today' (1993: 9). It is the sole serious question since to take it into account is also to change the very terms and conditions through which 'wars, conflicts ... debates, even passions' can be approached (1993: 9). It is not simply that death is a serious matter, but rather that the real it marks in this instance *as real* is vital. What it marks for Lyotard, as for Lacan, is the limits of what we know as not all there is.

For Lyotard, the real conceived of in this way – as real and so beyond the grasp of the imaginary and symbolic – is most definitely not a referent or metaphysical truth. Rather, it serves to question the possibility and the scope of both. For Lacan, the real as *real* is precisely what makes the question possible: 'Truth is nothing other than that which knowledge can apprehend as knowledge only by setting its own ignorance to work' (2003: 328). Knowledge can see itself as knowledge only in the recognition that it is knowledge by virtue of not being real and, therefore, partial and inadequate. In any other scenario – the real as symbolic or imaginary – knowledge continues to reign supreme and to continue unquestioned as though it were truth.

As we saw in Chapter 4, cultural relativism also calls the truth status of knowledge to account for itself. In Lévinas' face-to-face encounter with the other, the consciousness of both may be opened to revision and transformation in the recognition that 'man' is not all one. But cultural relativism also has its problems. What Lévinas proposes, as Derrida points out, depends entirely on 'man's' consciousness of himself as such and any transformation that takes place, takes place only within the terms of that consciousness. This isn't intrinsically a bad idea but it is a limited one. It is limited not least because in neglecting to account for the subject as a complex and unstable entity traversed by unconscious forces by definition beyond grasp in the conscious, the subject is presumed as a seamless whole. What Lévinas missed, it could be argued, is the radical possibilities opened up by an account of the subject in its own fragility.

For Lacan, any account of the subject as tied to the imaginary and symbolic, without simultaneous inculcation in the real, also misses a radical opportunity for a more searching critique of its own limits. While Lacan pays a great deal of attention to the function and effect of both the imaginary and symbolic, his account of the subject does not discount the origin of the real of being from which the infant struggles into the place of the subject in meaning, and as a continuing effect within meaning. One implication of this account of the subject as an effect of the interdependent relation of imaginary, symbolic *and* real, is that the subject is never fully within any of its terms. Another is that in their interdependence, no single realm is itself entirely itself either since it too is marked by the trace of the others within.

In his depiction of the confluence of the orders of the imaginary, symbolic and real, Lacan invokes topology as a form of signification which, he suggests, avoids the tendency towards invoking a referent that everyday discourse seems to manifest. As was suggested in Chapter 4, the imaginary, symbolic and real sketched topologically, foregrounds the absolute interdependency of its three orders by foregrounding movement as both space and time. The borromean knot has neither origin nor destination, neither inside nor outside, and it is not possible within itself to extract one or other of the realms without taking apart the whole. As a topology of the subject, the borromean knot produces a concept of the subject as neither fully a thing-in-itself nor a thing fully within any differentiated realm. The subject, here, is rather a dynamic process, always in motion, delimited only by the confluence that is mapped there. That the real should form an integral part of that confluence, therefore, has within Lacan's schema, crucial consequences for thinking subjectivity.

Unlike the imaginary and symbolic, which are by necessity partial and incomplete for Lacan, the real is that which is full, not lacking to itself since it is precisely not what is made (in culture) but what *is* (the real). Anything said to be 'of' the real, comprehended in meaning, is therefore not real but merely what it is possible, in culture, to imagine or symbolize. If it can be grasped, then what is grasped is not, by Lacan's definition at least, *real*. In this sense, what the real is, is that which cannot be comprehended, and in its incomprehensibility functions to remind us that comprehension is just that – the systematic production of intelligibility limited in its terms by the terms of the system. In this sense, the real must be that which cannot be symbolized as well as what cannot be imagined. It is *not* ideology, even in ideology's pretense, to be real and as such can neither be confirmed nor denied, and it cannot be traversed. If it cannot be traversed, the real cannot operate in the service of any particular cultural interest, but it can continue to mark the inadequacies of all and every interest in culture's terms.

That the real marks a limit, in this sense, seems vital to cultural criticism since it also marks the impossibility of cultural systems of meaning and the values generated there to be either real or absolute in the sense of their being all there is. This doesn't prevent cultural criticism from engaging and contesting meaning, but it does insist that the intangibility of the real changes the terms of that engagement and contestation. It also, of course, prevents any form of cultural criticism from establishing its way as the only way in the guise of truth. In the face of the Cartesian dualism of mind and body, the real reminds us of the dangers of the choice. Where Žižek posits a choice – between the good and the bad, authentic and pseudo, between the real as absent and the real as present – Lacan refuses, as Antony Easthope points out, the 'brutal and traditional logic of the either/or':

> some of the most crucial work in contemporary thinking – in Heidegger, Adorno, Lévinas and Derrida – has concentrated on this necessary impasse. Is Lacan's solution – or are his solutions (since the unconscious is by nature contradictory) – satisfactory? Certainly, the relentless binary logic of an *either* 'in discourse' *or* 'coming from the real' is a much worse solution or, in fact, no solution at all.
>
> (Easthope 2002: 130)

As Easthope reminds us, then, to deconstruct the real as guarantor does not necessarily have to entail for cultural criticism the decision of casting it either as presence or absence. For Derrida, as we have already seen, the 'politics' of such a choice would be distinctly, 'unethical', since the radical gesture is never to close down the possibilities as yet unanticipated and certainly not to restrict those possibilities merely to the terms of the symbolic systems of culture. If we comprehend the real, if we produce it as intelligible within our terms, then we lose the radical challenge to our own knowledge of ourselves as final.

For another British cultural critic, the facility of the question the real poses is also paramount. In her analysis of culture and the real, the real for Catherine Belsey is not *a* real or one *version* of it rather than another, but *the* real is vital to cultural criticism for the 'domain of meaningless alterity' it marks. The real for Belsey:

> is not nature ... Nor is the real a fact ... Still less is it the truth, a foundation on which to base new laws or dogmas, or an alternative reality with which to contrast appearances. *On the contrary, the real is a question, not an answer.*
>
> (Belsey 2005: 14; emphasis added)

In this sense, it is the radical alterity that could neither be named nor grasped in the explorations of the issues of ethics and alterity in the preceding chapters. However, in its insistent pressure on their terrain it is that which makes both ethics and alterity vital issues.

The issue of the real

The real as simulation, the real as void, the real as real. Each matters since each has different implications, not simply for cultural criticism but also its relation to the world. The real as simulation carries the possibilities of the real as the impossible other of signification, as that to which signification can never refer since it can do so only within its own terms. For Baudrillard, simulation works as a self-referential system which produces reality as the illusion of the real, or as though it were present in the sign of the real. That the terms of simulation do not refer to anything but themselves, does not necessarily mean that there is not a world out there, merely that whatever is out there cannot be intelligible. It also means that whatever is out there is not *in* signification and in turn is not touched by signification. The simulacra are never real.

The real as void, on the other hand, displaces the problematic priority of the symbolic onto that of the imaginary. If the real is a void which the fantasies erected in the imaginary serve to disavow or to keep from me in order to keep me going, then it is difficult to see how any 'I' would go there at all. More than this, however, the real as void seems unnecessarily to make the real a hostage to ideology as a form of false consciousness out of which 'I' might break by seeing it for what it really is, even if that is nothing. For Žižek, following Descartes, we really are, or can be if we're brave enough, masters of all we survey. Eventually. I can be in control, particularly if I can 'think outside the box' of what is, and still continue to think. Ironically, what this account of the real retains is the sovereignty of the subject, since the subject buffeted by the defiles of signification, may experience sufficient control of meaning to see beyond it. In some ways, what Žižek offers to cultural criticism can be compared to what Morpheus offers Neo in *The Matrix*. In order to fully appreciate the picture Žižek draws, we too must take the red pill that will erase, or at least override, organic being.

Only in accounts of the real as that which *is*, and cannot be grasped, is the certainty of the subject radically displaced. If the real is what is independent of my idea of it, then the real continues to haunt and to trouble not just my own particular version of reality but the certainty by which I come to know (anything) in the first place. For cultural criticism, therefore, the real is indispensable.

Nowhere is this more focused in contemporary cultural criticism than on the terrain of the human and its radical other – the inhuman. One of the arguments made, by Lyotard, in relation to the desire to surmount the real as real, is that made about developments in biotechnologies designed to continue beyond the demise of the organic human. Artificial Intelligence, he suggests, can never reproduce *human* thought since it is pure logic devoid of the unpredictability or error of the incalculable trace of organic processes. Any idea that we can exchange the human for the conjunction of intelligence systems with organic machinic simulations is to miss altogether what the human *is*. What it is is neither one nor the other, not even the two conjoined, but rather the confluence of the trace which can neither be predicted nor mastered. Why that might matter is the question addressed in Chapter 6.

6 The Inhuman

- Why the inhuman?
- The 'proper' human
- The inhuman
- The 'improper' human
- The issue of the inhuman

Why the inhuman?

With the furore surrounding developments in biotechnology and artificial intelligence in our contemporary world, the issue of the inhuman can appear to be more sharply focused for human culture than it has ever been before.[1] Indeed, it seems that for cultural criticism the temptation to suggest that we live in a time when what it means to be human is on the verge of collapse, can be overwhelming, and apocalyptic visions of the future certainly do abound. From the much vaunted possibilities of full body human cloning, creating not just a new genetic class structure but also a whole new simulation of the human itself, to the seeming profundity of shifts in subjectivity in the web-like maps of narrative interaction created by hypertext and cybernetic simulations, the human can seem as if it is, for the very first time, up for grabs.

On the other hand, it seems equally plausible to suggest that thinking about the human – what it means to *be* human – has always been a pre-occupation of *being* human. Ontology, as a branch of philosophy which specifically addresses the question of being as being human, has been concerned with determining this at least since Plato in the West. And philosophy has not been alone in the project either. The figure of the inhuman as some monstrous other of the human set on destroying it, has graced the pages of literature since the medieval chronicles of Ralph of Coggeshall, the Cistercian monk who recorded fishermen catching in their nets a being that appeared to be half-man, half-fish (2006). Most notably, since the name of Frankenstein now circulates as a sign of the horror of the artificial in our current social imaginary, the issue of the inhuman as explored in the pages Mary Shelley's *Frankenstein* has long served as a trope of the inhuman and its problematic circulation in terms of human being.[2]

This presents cultural criticism with a series of paradoxes. The inhuman is both now and always already, and while it appears particular in each instance of its articulation, nonetheless remains troublingly possible wherever the human is stated as such. It is, if we think of it semantically, at once both a negation (*not* human) and a preposition, expressing the thing it appears not to be (the human). It is, then, neither 'properly' inside nor outside the human but bound paradoxically to the constitution of the human from the beginning. And, of course, the human becomes, in turn, bound to the inhuman in its constitution in difference. While paradoxes are necessarily difficult to grasp, it should become clear in the course of this chapter that when it comes to the issue of the inhuman, this is precisely the point. Indeed, the contention here is that the value of the inhuman to the field of cultural criticism lies not in definitions of it as such, but rather in a resolute refusal to accept the possibility of the inhuman as a thing capable of definition in its own right. What is at issue here is not what the inhuman may or may not be, but rather how different attempts to conceptualize it may function in the domain of cultural analysis.

The 'proper' human

One avenue of thinking of the human as an essence, is that which invokes for that essence a value of certainty from which all else stems. In these terms, what is proper to the human is not only given, but in turn governs accounts of cultural value within the terms of that given. An obvious instance of this might be the ways in which the term inhuman comes to circulate within cultures as the mark of all that the human is not. Torture as inhuman, indifference to suffering as inhuman, the will of the powerful over the weak as inhuman, all rely on a notion of the human as stable and incontrovertible as a thing-in-itself. But they also confirm that thing by expunging from its terms bad human behaviour. The result of course, is that torture, indifference and power, do not properly belong on the scene of the human but also implicitly that real humans do not engage in these things. The Nazi death camps, then, were the work of monsters who were not properly human and so the human is absolved of responsibility in that direction. The monstrous other outside of the human, rather than within it, guarantees the proper operation of the human as stable, full to itself rather than ambivalent, and so as naturally or inherently the marker of good from which proper human relations can come. As a stable essence, the human may guarantee accounts of social orders as either in tune with this human or oppressive towards it. However, in either case the social is conceived of as that which is outside of the human for the purpose of regulating it.

For the German philosopher Karl Marx, capitalism was alienating in the sense that it divided the being of being human against itself by imposing material conditions within which humanity was curtailed. What was at stake in capital then, was a process of systematic dehumanization. For cultural critics, such as Theodor Adorno (1903–69) and Walter Benjamin (1892–1940), whose projects were to theorize the alienating effects of culture in capitalist economies, the human in this sense of a potentiality already 'there' in the world which is systematically assailed by that world, forms an important touchstone for thinking. Writing in *PRISMS* in 1967, Adorno famously argued that there could be no poetry after Auschwitz, since the barbarity enacted in the sign of the camp 'corrodes all knowledge' by discounting the human within its terms (Adorno 1967: 34). Writing in *Illuminations* in 1955, Benjamin similarly claimed that the modern industrial intervention in the organic process of creating art which the machines of mechanical reproduction represented for him destroys the 'aura' both of art and of its effects on human consciousness (Benjamin 1999: 215).

For Adorno, then, cultural criticism marches dialectically towards what he terms barbarism in its 'absolute reification' of itself in 'self-satisfied contemplation' (Adorno 1967: 34). So long as cultural criticism ignores the real of the human condition in its intellectually detached speculations, then cultural criticism will remain an ally of the barbarism done to the human and so ultimately becomes barbaric itself.

For Benjamin, 'Mankind', once an object for contemplation in the Greek tradition of 'Olympian Gods', now risks destitution in the 'self-alienating' systems of both production and thought as merely self-referential. Where art has, for Benjamin, become the space in which the human's own destruction of itself can be experienced in the simulation of aesthetic pleasure, communism must respond by 'politicizing art' as a means by which the human may retrieve itself in contemplation of the veracity of the condition of the human as human rather than the alienated work of inauthentic machinic production (Benjamin 1999: 235).

For both, what is 'proper' to the human is lost not only in the defiles of signification but also in the social structures that arise from signification as an exercise of a 'will to power' which, in forgetting the 'proper' human, become inhuman. While it is difficult to pin down the 'proper' in these terms, it is nonetheless very definitely there as a positive force.[3]

Another more recent account of both the essence and essential force of the human is that given by the American political theorist Francis Fukuyama (1952 –). While writing with an interest in preserving the status quo of social organization in the West, and so defending its terms from the destabilization advocated by the cultural criticism for which Adorno and Benjamin stand, Fukuyama, nonetheless, grounds his analysis on the same conceptual terrain. What is interesting about Fukuyama's account, however, is the overtly conflicted project it attempts to pursue.

Writing in *Our Posthuman Future* in 2003, Fukuyama argues that the essence of the human is in danger of being wiped out by the 'consequences of the biotechnology revolution' in the later twentieth and early twenty-first centuries. This matters to Fukuyama since this is precisely, in his account of it, the essence upon which liberal democracy as America knows it, is built. Concerned primarily with politics, Fukuyama's overt interest lies in the ways in which biotechnological developments impact on our understanding of politics and of the political systems of culture. Within these terms, the potential for undermining the category of the human which biotechnology seems to threaten, has the capacity also to radically unsettle the grounds on which notions of rights, freedoms and democracy, are possible in the first place.

Interestingly here, rights, freedoms and democracy are made certain by their grounding in the human as itself, an unchanging principle of certainty. In order to preserve that certainty and the values it guarantees, however, Fukuyama opens it to an uncertain relativism he seeks to contest. The solid ground of the human becomes controvertible in the very strategy by which it is affirmed and as such it is strategically difficult to re-assert:

> The aim of this book is to argue that Huxley was right, that the most significant threat posed by contemporary biotechnology is the possibility that it will alter human nature and thereby move us into a 'posthuman' stage of history. This is important, I will argue, because human nature exists, is a meaningful concept, and has provided a stable continuity to our experience as a species. It is, conjointly with religion, what defines our most basic values. Human nature shapes and constrains the possible kinds of political regimes, so a technology powerful enough to reshape what we are will have possibly malign consequences for liberal democracy and the nature of politics itself.
>
> (Fukuyama 2003: 7)

Here, human nature is valuable because it is real. Moreover, it is valuable in its reality in that it founds and sustains proper political regimes. Political regimes in turn are guaranteed by their foundation in the stable real of the human. At the same time, however, that stability is under threat. The human is open to redefinition and with it the regimes of power it sustains. For Fukuyama, we must then defend the unalterable against the potential of its alterability because what is at stake is cultural value. This is clearly problematic in a number of ways.

In the first place, Fukuyama makes the real of the human a hostage from the start to the cultural value he defends. Far from an *a priori* to culture, the human is culture's 'proper' effect. As such, the incontrovertible human is no more than common sense as a proper and fitting agreement of a particular set of values. The human, then, is ideology. In the second place *as ideology* the human is, paradoxically, a form of false consciousness since, like religion, it serves to protect us from ourselves and so to maintain the experience of the social group in the idea of it. The fear that technology will move the human beyond itself is thereby the fear that the human was never itself, as such, in the first place. As cultural value rather than real, the human is not only open to critical engagement, but the task of de-instituting its authority to govern the way things are, seems more urgent than ever. Fukuyama's anxious iteration of the human in the place of the real is, therefore, the seed of its own downfall. In the end, for Francis Fukuyama, the consequences of de-instituting his notion of the human are clear in cultural terms. Anything which calls into question the stable human essence he invokes also calls into question the liberal democratic ideal of the United States of America, which it sustains as truth.

It is not difficult to suggest that the human values enshrined in the ideal of the US constitution – that all men are created equal and have unalienable rights by virtue of their humanity – is not entirely an ideal tied to value rather than any singular form of truth grounded in the real:

> The American regime was built, beginning in 1776, on a foundation of natural right. Constitutional government and a rule of law, by limiting the arbitrary authority of tyrants, would protect the kind of freedom that human beings by nature enjoyed ...
>
> So, despite the poor repute in which concepts like natural rights are held by academic philosophers, much of our political world rests on the existence of a stable human 'essence' with which we are endowed by nature, or rather, on the fact that we believe such an essence exists.
>
> We may be about to enter into a posthuman future, in which technology will give us the capacity gradually to alter that essence over time.
>
> (Fukuyama 2003: 216–17)

There is a desperate need, Fukuyama urges, to return to a pre-Kantian tradition that grounds rights and morality in nature (2003: 112).[4] But nature returns persistently to the 'contemporary capitalist liberal democratic institutions' which have the measure of the real most realistically. While Marx might have agreed with Fukuyama on the principle of the human as conceptual possibility, his idea of the outcome of making that conceptual move is undoubtedly less favourable to the notion of capitalism as the right, because natural, state of things. If the constitutional government of the USA is right because it is natural, then not only is there no hope of contesting its terms, but any other way of organizing human culture is morally wrong. This may go some way towards accounting for the fantasy of mastery in America's absolute sense of its relation to the other in its own idea of the world, but the totality it represents is surely in urgent need of interrogation.

What is 'proper' to the human, or the 'proper-ness' of the human, must be one place from which to start such interrogation. But this interrogation itself also begins to point to a far deeper problem with the concept of the human as stable essence, which continues beyond what is either proper or improper to it. The problem with the human in these terms then, is the conceptual problem of presence. On this terrain, the inhuman may have something to contribute to the de-institution of the human but not at all by simply replacing it.

The inhuman

One philosopher whose work has consistently addressed the question of the metaphysics of presence is, of course, Jacques Derrida. Writing in the first chapter of *Of Grammatology* under the heading 'The written being/the being written', Derrida reminds us that the question of being has also always been the question of its limits:[5]

> 'being,' as it is fixed in its general syntactic and lexicological forms within linguistics and Western philosophy, is not a primary and absolutely irreducible signified, that it is still rooted in a system of languages and an historically determined 'significance,' although strangely privileged as the virtue of disclosure and dissimulation.
>
> (Derrida 1976: 23)

Here, 'being' will always elude its fixing in metaphysics in part, because it has always been open to change. If we think of being in global and historical terms, it is clear that what it comes to signify is different in different cultural contexts and has changed over time. But 'being' will always elude attempts to fix it because it is always already in part an effect of the movement of signification through difference. That is, 'being' is thought, conceptually, not on the basis of what it *is*, but rather as an effect of the distribution of what is and what is not. In this way, the human – the being of being-human – is not simply contained in the category of the human established for all time. Moreover, as an effect of the operation of difference, the category of the human radically depends for its constitution, as such, on the category of that which is not human in order that it may be defined by its difference to it. In this account, far from constituting a transcendental signified, the human is always already split – it is radically divided by the trace of the other that constitutes it. The human, understood as a category in this way, is also always prefigured by that which it is not, and so where the human is, its other will always be. This makes the human a possible category of thought, but also immediately an unstable one. Shot through by that which is not human, the human is eternally haunted by the spectre of something other than itself, even from the very moment of its inception.

For Derrida, as has been noted elsewhere in this book, revealing the impossible logic of difference is not the end of analysis but rather the beginning of an alternative practice of critical engagement. Once identified, the operation of difference can be 'inhabited' by analysis which serves to draw out both the possibilities and the simultaneous impossibilities of the values emerging from that operation. This is what Derrida, as we explored it in Chapter 4, terms 'differance' (with an 'a'). Neither a concept nor a thing, the operation of differance may be traced as the play which both inaugurates and unsettles difference.

This may be the difference of signification or the difference of the conscious, but it may also be the difference of being in relation to both. For Derrida, 'differance' may be thought differently in each instance of its operation within the symbolic as signification, the human in its consciousness of self and within the ontology of human Being. Thus signification is not reducible to consciousness and neither signification nor consciousness is reducible to being. Differance plays across them and in some ways, their confluence is also the confluence where differance is most urgently at work. Writing specifically of being in 'differance', Derrida notes for example that:

> Being has always made 'sense', has always been conceived or spoken of as such, only by dissimulating itself in beings; thus, in a particular and very strange way, differance (is) 'older' than the ontological difference or the truth of Being ... It is a trace that no longer belongs to the horizon of Being but one whose sense of Being is borne and bound by this play; it is a play of traces or difference that has no sense and is not, a play that does not belong. There is no support to be found and no depth to be had for this bottomless chessboard where Being is set in play.
>
> (Derrida 1973: 154)

Differance, then, is older than Being. Being, as intelligible, comes about through the play of differance which marks both the trace of the other within the self-same, and at the same time, the limits of both. Importantly, the support that is to be found for Being is *not* located in presence. But, then again, it cannot be located in absence either. Being is rather always already the play of differance. Established through the play of the trace, the category of the human is always unstable even in the very moment of its inception as such.

Being in meaning is always tremulous since it seems always to carry the possibility within it that at any moment it can be undone. While such an undoing would not necessarily be a radical gesture, on the contrary it would literally be unthinkable, it does go some way towards accounting for the anxiety about otherness that cultures display. Anxiety, in this sense of it, may well be focused in the direction of biotechnologies or robotic simulations in our contemporary, but it is by no means initiated by them since it had manifested itself differently before those technologies and we have no reason to assume that it won't continue beyond them, no matter how particular those technologies may appear to be. If differance is older than being, then the initiation of being on the grounds of its play is always already uncertain. Any priority accorded the human will always be lacking, but then so too will any priority accorded the non-human as the absence of the fully present human.

Differance is older than being, then, in the sense that being is an intelligible category of meaning and is, therefore, at work in order that the being assigned to beings may be possible in the first place. But differance is also older than being in the sense that what it means to be – to experience, to think, to be in being – is itself always already divided, always already neither fully present nor absent, but strung somewhere within the simultaneous play of both. Derrida elaborates this in his rereadings of some of Freud's work on the unconscious, but particularly in his reading of Freud's mystic writing pad as was noted in Chapter 1. Here what separates the human from the machine is not the definitive priority of the human in its presence as such, but rather paradoxically the condition of the human as neither fully present nor absent. The human in these terms is possible in the ambivalent play of the neither/nor.

For Jean-François Lyotard, it is precisely that play that provides the possibility of the continued existence of the human, even in the face of the desire to erase it in the desire for certainty that some biotechnologies appear to offer. The premise of such technologies, Lyotard suggests, is to master the lack inherent within the human, by technologically enhancing the human to an imagined point of perfection. Here, perfection equates to a certainty of presence that is always already impossible. It is a fantasy for Lyotard which in its dream of escaping the ambivalence of being in meaning ironically returns the human to the realms of the real in the form of annihilation. This fantasy of escape from the symbolic is one of the issues explored by Lyotard in his extended work on the inhuman, which we began to address in relation to the question of the real in the preceding chapter.

In this work, Lyotard distinguishes between two forms of the inhuman which, he argues, it 'is indispensable to keep apart' (1994: 2). Writing in the form of a question, he asks:

> What if human beings, in humanism's sense, were in the process of, constrained into, becoming inhuman (that's the first part)? And (the second part), what if what is 'proper' to humankind were to be inhabited by the inhuman?
>
> (Lyotard 1994: 2)

The first part of this proposition suggests a movement beyond the human, a transformation of both the concept of the human, 'in humanism's sense', and of the being of being human 'becoming inhuman'. This is also exterior, in that the human here is assailed from the outside, altered, corrupted by matter which does not belong to it but comes from elsewhere. This could be capitalism, or technology, or, simply, the alienating system of language and culture. The second part of the proposition, on the other hand, suggests interiority, a 'haunting' of the human by an 'other' at once both intrinsic and alien to it. The human here is always already inhabited from within, as if in the constitution of its humanness there remains an excess, a contradiction, something which troubles the smooth running of the being of being human as a very condition of its possibility in the first place.

At first glance, it may seem that the two are not mutually exclusive. For Lyotard, however, it is important to 'dissociate' them, since each gives rise to a different set of possibilities both for thinking the human–inhuman relation and for what he calls a 'radical politics', within which our very existence as human is understood to be the stake (1994: 4). As long as we continue to think of the human as simply assailed from outside, we are in danger, Lyotard argues, of complicity with the destruction of the human as such.

There is no essence of the human for Lyotard since what the human is, is not grounded in a unity or even the potentiality of fullness to itself sought from the supplement that may one day complete it. The logic of the supplement, following Derrida, is not that which adds to the positivity of presence, but that which substitutes for its lack by marking its absence as such (Derrida 1976: 145).

For Lyotard, then, the technology intended to redress the lack of the subject merely passes it by, by bypassing the conditions by which the subject gets to be subject in the first place. In exchanging the subject for being as though both were the same thing, the fantasy of technology also, ironically, renders the real of the human redundant. If there is something proper to the human, Lyotard argues, it is not that which can be grasped in our consciousness of it no matter how complex that consciousness becomes. The proper of the human in this sense is not simply a matter of intelligibility:

> What we shall call human in humans, the initial misery of their childhood, or their capacity to acquire a 'second' nature which, thanks to language, makes them fit to share in communal life, adult consciousness and reason? That the second depends on and presupposes the first is agreed by everyone. The question is only that of knowing whether this dialectic, whatever name we grace it with, leaves no remainder.
>
> (Lyotard 1994: 3)

Here, what is 'proper' to the human inheres neither in its consciousness nor its materiality. It is neither the capacity to think, nor the mechanics of its organic being. It is, in other words, not simply reducible either to its soft- or its hardware in technology's terms. The misery of childhood, the alienation of being in meaning produce the human, but the very condition of its production in these terms renders the human ambivalent. Whatever name we grace the process with, the point of contest is the remainder. If there is none, then machines can replicate the being of being human. If there is, then they cannot. For Lyotard, the remainder, not the alienation, is the key. Here the second form of the inhuman, as he began by defining it, comes to the fore. That is, the inhuman which unsettles from within, and from which there is no escape.

What is 'proper' to the human, in these terms, is what is also proper to any form of biological life for Lyotard, some form of organic embodiment. While this may, in part, be intelligible within the symbolic – within the terms of what we know – it also belongs ultimately to the real, which will in the end return to claim it. No matter how much we conceptualize either the possibility or the impossibility of the category of the human, the very question itself will disappear with the death of the sun. As organic material, no animal life will survive the event. And this will be real in the Lacanian sense. It will *not* depend on anyone's idea of it. Old distinctions, those of man and animal, original and copy, real and artificial, will cease to carry value since they will not survive, at least not organically. Should they survive by virtue of their simulation – in artificial intelligence housed in robotic simulations of life – they will not be human, since they will remain trapped fully within the logic of each system. Without synthesis, and the unpredictable excesses generated in the confluence of imaginary, symbolic and real, that being human is for Lyotard, each element of being beyond the human will not continue to be human since it will refer only to itself.

As an illusion of perfection, this marks for Lyotard the dangers of thinking that we know and, therefore, control the world devoid of a real that is engendered only in our idea of it. What is 'X'd out' of our writings will indeed return to consume 'us'. While Lyotard's reflections on the inhuman remind us of the vitality of an account of organic matter, however, they do not return us simply to the realms of a simple 'real of the body'. What he offers is far from the dualism of the mind–body split. Indeed, there are none of the comforts of the humanism in this account that his work as a whole seeks to displace.[6] Finally, the human is *not* for Lyotard since it is not simply reducible to a thing. The human is not an essence, nor is it manifest in a dialectically organized relation between thought and matter. Rather, and somewhat ironically, what is 'proper' to the human is exactly its displacement in the movement of an impossible desire to overcome it.[7]

Not only is the human displaced from the certainty of presence, then, but that displacement in turn motivates a desire to recuperate a form of presence which *is* fully present to itself and so lacking nothing. Once again, this is precisely the condition of being in meaning analysed by Lacan on the terrain of the subject. Founded in lack, the subject in Lacan's terms is destined to seek but never to find the 'thing' that will end its uncertainty to itself once and for all. 'Desire,' he writes in the *Écrits*, 'is the metonymy of the want to be' (2003: 286). Here, desire is the desire to overcome the movement of signification that founds meaning in difference and so bring the lack of being under control by filling it with something else.

That this is possible only metonymically has two major consequences for the subject. The first is that what we desire will never make good the lack originating in the separation from being in meaning since it will always emerge for the subject from a place within meaning. The second is that desire, as a result, is always impossible and so endlessly unfulfillable. The one thing that the subject lacks and can never make good is the unity of presence full to itself, and so complete in itself, that we left behind in being for the promise of meaning. What the subject seeks, then, is a return to being in the fullness of the real, but were that to be achieved in any literal sense, the subject would no longer be possible even to itself. Desire as metonymy troubles the subject but also maintains its possibility of articulating that trouble as a question within meaning.

That desire is troubling for the subject points to the condition of being human in the world of meaning as a condition which, as noted in the preceding chapter, comes about in the confluence of Lacan's three orders of imaginary, symbolic and real. Here, the real continues as a trace of that which the subject cannot grasp but which, while not 'there' for the subject in its consciousness, is nonetheless still 'out there'. For Lacan, the subject is 'a hole surrounded by something'. One metaphor for this in the broader project of his work, is that of the vase created on a potter's wheel. Writing in *The Ethics of Psychoanalysis,* for example, Lacan suggests that:

> if you consider the vase from the point of view I first proposed, as an object made to represent the existence of emptiness at the centre of the real that is called the Thing, this emptiness as represented in representation presents itself as *nihil*, as nothing. And that is why the potter, just like you to whom I am speaking, creates the vase with his hand around this emptiness, creates it, just like a mythical creator, *ex nihilo*, starting with a hole.
>
> (Lacan 1992: 121)

Here, the subject is made in language like an object lost to signification and the remainder of being abandoned in the real represents itself in meaning as the intangible thing of nihil. Unavailable to meaning, being appears in meaning as nothing. While the subject 'creates' a something around the emptiness which founds it in signification, it does so only in the emptiness of the sign. In this sense, the Thing that the subject seeks is motivated by the trace of that which is lost, and at the same time unknown. The paradox, of course, is that both motivation and seeking are incompatible with the Thing itself, since they are only possible from the 'side' of meaning as represented by Lacan in the Venn diagram of Being *or* Meaning. The subject only 'knows' that something is lost within the symbolic terms that make 'knowing' possible. As 'fabricated signifier' (1992: 122), the Thing is not imaginary, symbolic or real, but rather held in tension in the confluence of the borromean knot:

> I referred last time to the schematic example of the vase, so as to allow you to grasp where the Thing is situated in the relationship that places man [*sic*] in the mediating function between the real and the signifier. This Thing, all forms of which created by man belong to the sphere of sublimation, this Thing will always be represented by emptiness, precisely because it cannot be represented by anything else – or, more exactly, because it can only be represented by something else. But in every form of sublimation, every form of emptiness is determinative.
>
> (Lacan 1992: 129–30)

Situated in a relationship that places 'man' in a mediating function between the real and the signifier, then, the Thing is ambivalently both inside the place of man as subject, but also exterior to it in the place of the subject in the order of the signifier. And, it is precisely this ambivalence that for Lacan makes the human subject human. The trace of being in the real, while we cannot know it as a particular thing, is nonetheless the very 'thing' that, beyond comprehension, distinguishes the human subject from its machinic simulation. While the robot is made fully within the knowledge of the symbolic and the imaginary, the human subject alone retains the trace of a radical alterity from which it cannot escape, no matter what its desires in that direction.

Desire is, then, neither organic being nor symbolic systems but rather a movement arising from the complex confluence of imaginary, symbolic and real. In this sense, desire marks the condition of human being in the world. It marks the difference between human and machine, but does so without determining the inhuman as belonging properly on one side or other of the binary that allows for the possibility of thinking the relation in the first place. The inhuman for Lacan is always already within, of and founding, the human rather than something which comes from outside in order to outstrip the human. The elusive thing is the thing that cannot be either grasped or overcome.

For Lyotard, the issue of embodiment focused by technological developments in the later twentieth century that allow for a range of prostheses from arms to kidneys, arises both from the fragility of organic matter, but also from the desire to overcome the temporality of being in an organic sense. To be human, for Lyotard, is to be irrevocably haunted by the spectre of the inhuman thing as a trace of the trauma that coming into meaning from being in the real necessarily entails. In answer to his own question, 'Can thought go on without a body?' Lyotard's answer in the negative is unequivocal.

The 'improper' human

For a number of cultural critics, the ambivalent uncertainty of the human inhabited by the inhuman is just too much to bear. Recognizing an urgent need to interrogate the limits of a humanism which places an unproblematic natural human at its centre, a variety of cultural critiques seek to move beyond the certainty of that human to somewhere else which does not need to take account of it. Here the 'improper' human exceeds the conservative limits of humanism's human by staking its 'badly behaving human' to the terrain of the inhuman. The inhuman thus becomes the properly functioning sign of a different sort of human condition. For the writing team of the philosopher Gilles Deleuze (1925–95) and the psychoanalyst Félix Guattari (1930–92), the answer to Lyotard's question is equally unequivocal. Not only *can* thought go on without a body, but if the human is to escape its cruel curtailment in symbolic law, then it *must*.

The work of Deleuze and Guattari is explicitly dedicated to the project of exploring the status of 'the concept' in philosophy, in relation to what they call the chaos of life (2003). That chaos, it seems, emerges as a condition of the random flows of psychic phenomena unregulated by any form of submission to law. While for Lyotard, thought is an effect of the trauma of moving from being to meaning in the foundation of the subject, for Deleuze and Guattari, thought is a radically unanchored flux independent of a subject and, as such, always in a process of becoming. Resisting an account of the human in terms of the subject, the being which emerges as an effect of this analysis is posited as a self.

The figure of this self is the figure of what they term the 'schizo' as an attempt to designate, without fixing, a web-like terrain of thought unhindered by law. In order to do this, Deleuze and Guattari rely on a series of reworkings of terms drawn from elsewhere. Prominent among these are rhizome (a term in plant biology for the root systems of tubers), desire (from Lacan but not of Lacan), machine (from Lyotard's techno-science but not of that science), and becoming (from Heidegger's distinction between Being and being-in-the-world, though not fully of that either). Their work in this sense is an eclectic fusion of misbehaving concepts which as they define them, are never simple. Indeed, writing in *What Is Philosophy?* Deleuze and Guattari are clear that concepts are not static or determined things, but rather open, moving, temporal points in networks they create but which also extend beyond them: 'There are no simple concepts. Every concept has components and is defined by them. It therefore has a combination [*chiffre**]. It is a multiplicity, although not every multiplicity is conceptual' (Deleuze and Guattari 2003: 15). As the asterix suggests, even this definition eludes definition. The translator's note points out that there are many, often difficult, English translations of 'chiffre' including, 'figure', 'numeral', 'sum total', 'initials' or 'monogram', 'secret code' or 'cipher' (2003: ix). Concepts then are to define the terrain, but the terrain thus defined will always exceed its definition. It will always, in other words, move on, and in so doing begin again anew. This movement, understood both temporally and spatially in this work, is also a significant component of it. Concerned to understand what things are, Deleuze and Guattari suggest that we must understand their duration. That is, while there are *things*, while there is an *is* to existence in their terms, it is only comprehensible in time and space and then only fleetingly, marked not by its essence but rather by its *time*.

A rhizome is a continuously growing root, which is not quite a root in the conventional sense, since it puts out shoots at intervals only to move on again in different directions. It is, then, always on the move, always growing and doing so laterally rather than by linear progression. It is also an effect of chance rather than design or inherent nature. As such, the rhizome provides a useful metaphor for the mobile concept of thought posited by Deleuze and Guattari. Unstructured by law, nothing is necessarily taboo for the human. As a result, thought is potentially endless, and, since it is not in reference to structures external to itself, randomly and transiently productive. Rhizomatic thought emphasizes connections devoid of centres and foundations. It is not a result of a process either inherent to the nature of mind or to that of organic being, but rather a viral-like network of possibilities generating other possibilities devoid of design. In this sense, rhizomatic thinking outlives the human in humanism's sense. With no ground and no inherent boundaries, it is pure simulacra. There is no truth to the rhizome because there is no essence to the rhizome. It *is*, but only in the time of its becoming. And, then, it is something else.

For Deleuze and Guattari, this is a perfect metaphor for being unfettered by anything grounded as real, even, ironically, being itself. The real for them is the propaganda of the system, and we need not submit to it. By proliferating the flow of life in the image of the rhizome, we can thus escape the bounds of subjection to which that system submits being in its structures of being-in-the-world. Here, being is not the foundation. It is not a something which is alienated in culture, but rather a something which always escapes any constitution as such. In this sense, being *as* rhizome becomes the eternal process of becoming without ever arriving. And, that, it seems, is precisely the point. To arrive is to be done with the process and by implication to be done with the rhizome. The rhizome is at once both becoming and the impossibility of becoming which are both, potentially, endless: 'A becoming is not a correspondence between relations. But neither is it a resemblance, an imitation, or, at the limit, an identification ... Becoming produces nothing other than itself,' (Deleuze and Guattari 2004b: 262). Understood semantically, becoming in this sense operates as a verb with 'a consistency all of its own' (2004b: 263). It cannot be reduced to, or trace an origin in, 'appearing', 'being', 'equaling' or 'producing' (2004b: 263). It is an action, then, but a subject-less one, neither instigated nor resulting in anything which is not itself.

If it is transcendent in this way, however, 'becoming' is not fully present to itself, since it is a process without end. Like Lacan's conceptualization of 'desire', it can never be fulfilled. Unlike Lacan's conception of desire, however, becoming has no relation to either the symbolic or the real, the conflict of which, for Lacan, initiates it.

In part, becoming is not desire in the Lacanian sense, since it has no reference to anything outside of itself, especially the body. Significantly, where the body does appear in Deleuze and Guattari, it appears as a virtual network devoid of the usual limits which embodiment might otherwise suggest. It is, most famously, a 'body without organs' (2004a: 9–17). That is, it is not driven by need, demand or desire. The body without organs is not determined by its component parts, nor is it restricted to them. It is not, in Deleuze and Guattari's terms, filiated to the material organic being which the body is conceived as being. If there is a 'body', it is, paradoxically, a momentary and random assemblage of unrelated and so dis-assemble-able parts. It is not, in this sense, organic and it is certainly not in any permanent relation to thought. But the body without organs is also, of course, without need in that there is nothing symbolically upon which it depends in order to exist as such. It is the body without demand, since it has no destination. And, it is the body without desire as a drive governed phenomenon, since it has neither need nor demand. Can thought go on without a body for Deleuze and Guattari? Absolutely.

This is appealing, since it augurs a freedom from the strictures of social order for those oppressed, or alienated, by them. And, in this respect, the body without organs is significant in one further respect. Without organs, the body is not differentiated. Or, if it is differentiated, difference is limitless and endlessly multiplying, endlessly producing difference itself. The body without organs, then, is also the body without sex, or at least the body without sexual difference. *This* body escapes the play of the masculine and feminine upon which others, including Lacan, have argued that signification in the metaphysics of the West is founded.[8] Since there is no founding difference, the body is without restraint. While this does seem to offer plentiful possibilities for disrupting the being of being-in-the-world in gendered terms, however, it does rely on both a notion of evading metaphysics by stepping outside it and of the possibility of doing both by freeing the mind of the shackles of intelligibility that metaphysics suggests. Ironically, gender here becomes nothing more than our idea of it and any response to gender as difference or the value inscribed there has recourse only to a place outside of metaphysics which is the place of a natural flow of life forces. Undifferentiated, the body can be made and made again as a random set of possibilities. Here gender as gender belongs only to the force of law and therefore has no relation to any real. Menstruation, presumably, has no place there since in the ideal of a beyond of metaphysics we will no longer 'know' it. I have reservations.

One way in which the work of Deleuze and Guattari moves away from the organic embodiment of the body central to humanism, towards the unfettered ideal of the random network, is through the image of the machine. Writing about cinema as a particular technology of experience, Deleuze and Guattari argue that film is already 'machinic' in that it frees the eye from the body and any process of interpretation determined by the observer within the bounds of whom the eye may be said to function. In this sense, cinema is an entirely visceral experience in that it promotes the raw experience of sensation over sense as organized, structured, thought. But the machine is not limited in their work to any literal technological interpretation and rather nomadically comes to operate in the place of more conventional concepts of the process of thought itself.

Devoid of the organic as determining, thought can no longer be conceived as that which is founded in, or bounded by, recourse to a logic of the whole. Here, the metaphor of the human is redundant, since it carries too many connotations of gestalt, of intent, of purpose and destiny. The human gets replaced in this schema by the metaphor of the machine. The idea of machines, in contrast to that of humans, does not depend on the organic and so is not invested with any reason to be either whole or foundational. Machines, after all, have no identity, no destiny and no end. They are, simply, component parts, responding only to input which has nothing whatever to do with 'them'. In this sense, of course, machines for Deleuze and Guattari are not the material phenomena of technology, but rather an idea of virtual possibilities. 'Machinic enslavement', they argue, must be kept separate from 'social subjection':

> There is enslavement when human beings themselves are constituent parts of a machine that they compose among themselves and with other things (animals, tools), under the control and

> direction of a higher unity. But there is subjection when the higher unity constitutes the human being as a subject linked to a now exterior object, which can be animal, a tool or even a machine.
>
> (Deleuze and Guattari 2004b: 504)

Enslavement is not subjection, then, since the submission it entails is *internal* to the human and not the result of *external* force. Of course, enslavement is still enslavement and, as Deleuze and Guattari go on to insist, this distinction between the machine and the human does not imply any further distinction between good or bad forms. At the same time, however, the distinction between internal and external is intriguing, particularly in the context of a liberation which does not depend on a notion of a whole. For enslavement, as a verb, to be capable of being distinguished in terms of an inside and outside, reduces the 'tetravalent' assemblage to the notion of two (2004b: 98). Perhaps not quite a dualism, inside and outside still function here as what seems to be the proper and improper of the human traversed.

And that, in the end, is the point of the analysis which Deleuze and Guattari offer. For the human to be productive and not enslaved, what is 'proper' to the human must be divested in its 'improper' possibilities. It entails a move away from organic and humanist models of the human to become inhuman, what Deleuze and Guattari call 'Desiring-Machines' (2004a: 1).

Desiring-Machines are neither driven by law nor curtailed by it:

> It is at work everywhere, functioning smoothly at times, at other times in fits and starts. It breathes, it heats, it eats. It shits and fucks. What a mistake to have ever said *the* id. Everywhere *it* is machines – real ones, not figurative ones: machines driving other machines, machines being driven by other machines, with all the necessary couplings and connections. An organ-machine is plugged into an energy-source-machine: the one produces a flow that the other interrupts. The breast is a machine that produces milk, and the mouth a machine coupled to it. The mouth of the anorexic wavers between several functions: its possessor is uncertain as to whether it is an eating-machine, an anal machine, a talking-machine, or a breathing machine (asthma attacks). Hence, we are all handymen: each with his little machines. For every organ-machine, an energy machine: all the time, flows and interruptions.
>
> (Deleuze and Guattari 2004a: 1)

If there is a substance to machines, then, it is a substance internal only to the machine itself and is manifest only in a notion of 'function'. While the machine eats, shits and fucks, these are merely functions of the machine. But they are also functional in the sense that all that the machine does is organized around being able to eat, shit and fuck. Further, the relation of the machine to other machines is also functional. It is an external effect of either 'driving' or 'being driven'. One machine may give rise to the function of another, but it will also be transformed by the connection made. Each depends on the energy of the other and where it is buffeted depends merely on random interactions or collisions. In addition, the function of the machine, while perhaps internally and temporarily determined, can never be delimited by anything like intent. At the same time, however, the functions of the machine are literal, they cannot signify anything other than themselves. If the machine eats, shits and fucks, these are functions rather than signs. Eating relates only to other functions, it is not a cathexis of pleasure. Similarly, shitting and fucking are shitting and fucking. They cannot be the metonymy of pleasure, fantasy, pain or fear.

In Deleuze and Guattari's image of the machine, there is no superego that either controls or holds together the assemblage that constitutes it. Rather, in its place is desire as a Nietzschean 'will to power', devoid of organs and constituted solely in terms of internal function. But function itself is never wholly determined either. It is always open to misdirected effects, since while it is internal to the singularity of any given machine, it can only be manifest, as such, in a dependent relation to the conditions presented by the proximity of other machines. One 'will to power' will necessarily succumb to another and so change the course of its flow. Function, then, may begin as one thing and continue as something else altogether, since it is undelimited by interest or investment of a singular kind. That the breast is a machine that produces milk in these terms seems a particularly stark example of dis-investment. It is hard to imagine the breast as object but not of the desire born of a displacement or cathexis of sexual difference.

Taking the image of the machine as literally as it is depicted in the opening pages of *Anti-Oedipus* (Deleuze and Guattari (2004b)), explorations of the possibilities of machinic existence in terms of robotics and prosthetics, is an avenue explored by a number of theorists concerned with the category of the body as defined by the figure of the Cyborg. Interestingly, though they are not all addressed specifically to the work of Deleuze and Guattari, all, nonetheless, entail a similar disavowal of sexual difference, and of the signification of things beyond their existence as functions. Perhaps the most noted of these is Donna J. Haraway's 'Cyborg Manifesto' (1991).

Writing in *Simians, Cyborgs and Women: The Reinvention of Nature*, Haraway (1965–) puts forward a manifesto in which she describes both the state of 'Science, technology, and socialist feminism in the late twentieth century', and offers the possibilities of ways out of that state which will benefit the project of socialist feminism. As with Fukuyama's later 'posthuman future', Haraway's manifesto is interestingly conflicted. It is at once, she claims, 'irony', 'myth', 'blasphemy' and, thus, interrogative, questioning by destabilizing the structures of authority which sustain literal meanings, reality and, finally, the discourse of religion and the transcendent figurehead of God. But, at the same time, it is also a manifesto and so manifestable, achievable, even real. It is distinguishable, she insists, from 'apostasy' (1991: 149). While interrogating religious belief, then, it also maintains its own religiosity.

A cyborg is, Haraway asserts:

> a cybernetic organism, a hybrid of machine and organism, a creature of social reality as well as a creature of fiction ... The cyborg is a matter of fiction and lived experience that changes what counts as women's experience in the late twentieth century. This is a struggle over life and death, but the boundary between science fiction and social reality is an optical illusion.
>
> (Haraway 1991:149)

The cyborg is real and fictional, it is a matter of lived experience and it changes what counts as women's experience. It marks a struggle (over life and death) but also the dissolution of a boundary (between science fiction and social reality). The cyborg, then, is the figure of escape. It dismantles the reality of social existence, particularly as it manifests sexual difference, and it replaces that reality with a fiction, or an imaginary which, while virtual, is also a better version of the real, understood as the capacity of experience. The cyborg's escape is not just an escape from the limits of traditional categories of thought which curtail women's experience, however, it is also an escape to a different plane: that of the virtual. Having no foundations other than those of fiction, this virtual still provides a foundation for a new social order. An order that is, which creates 'a world without gender', 'a world without genesis', and 'a world without end' (Haraway 1991: 150).

Located in a time of a future yet-to-come, this is also a world in which pleasure is thought to abound, but not without responsibility. While pleasure here is the pleasure of confusing the boundaries, it is also a responsibility in constructing boundaries anew (1991: 150). It is not, therefore, the rhizomatic schizoid networks imagined by Deleuze and Guattari, nor the postmodern condition characterized by the internal implosion of grand narratives of legitimation theorized in Lyotard. Rather, it is the socialist-feminist goal driven project of dismantling '**phallogocentrism**' (1991: 176).

It would, of course, be crass to suggest that the project of dismantling 'phallogocentrism' is not one which is at least worth thinking about. But there is a problem with implicating that project in the figure of the cyborg as Haraway imagines it here. This becomes still more problematic by the location of the cyborg in the peculiar time of our now. The argument, clearly, is that the realities of artificial intelligence and artificial life once languishing in the imagination of science fiction, afford an opportunity for socialist feminism which can be positively seized. But, it doesn't work like that. By stating the argument in these terms, phallogocentrism is left to proliferate. That is, the 'what is' of phallogocentrism is simply sidestepped and in the process a different kind of opportunity for engaging its terms is lost. Phallogocentrism, in this account of it, is far more omnipotent than it needs to be. Here it simply *is*, as a condition with which we must live until the fantastical possibility of another form of living happens to emerge. As a possibility which is an effect of 'our time' rather than an enduring condition of its own impossibility at the heart of phallogocentrism from the start, the cyborg merely represents a form of escape which leaves the very terms and conditions of phallogocentrism rather firmly in place. This matters precisely because a move beyond metaphysics to a place free from its curtailment, even if it were possible, is not an engagement with metaphysics which will challenge its terms. It is not, in other words, a radical gesture since it leaves that which it claims to transcend very firmly in place.

This is intimated early in Haraway's arguments as she states that: 'By the late twentieth century, our time, a mythic time, we are all chimeras, theorized and fabricated hybrids of machine and organism, in short, we are cyborgs. The cyborg is our ontology' (1991: 150). Perhaps I have the benefit of hindsight, but I see no examples of the chimeras we have all become. That the 'cyborg is our ontology', merely replaces one form of ontology for another. It replaces the human with another form of the human, and in so doing does nothing whatever to challenge the ontological status of the human as such.

This is finally made clear in the conclusion of the manifesto, where the cyborg emerges as a 'powerful infidel heteroglossia':

> Cyborg imagery can suggest a way out of the maze of dualisms in which we have explained our bodies and our tools to ourselves. This is a dream not of a common language, but of a powerful infidel heteroglossia. It is an imagination of a feminist speaking in tongues to strike fear into the circuits of the supersavers of the new right. It means both building and destroying machines, identities, categories, relationships, space stories. Though both are bound in the spiral dance, I would rather be a cyborg than a goddess.
>
> (Haraway 1991: 181)

The cyborg is imaginary, and in that, the cyborg is the power to transcend the state of what is. It takes us out of the 'maze of dualisms' which 'explains us'. If ever there were an argument for the Cartesian *cogito*, this is it. Haraway may well prefer the cyborg to the goddess, I'm happy to continue with unsettling the dualism upon which such a choice depends.

There is another way of thinking the relation between women and the viral-like networks of communication opened up by information technology in recent years. Through the metaphor of 'Zeros' and 'Ones', in her analysis of 'Digital women and the new technoculture' (1998), for example, Sadie Plant (1964 –) extends the analysis of gender as predicated on presence and absence which was begun by French feminist theorists, such as Hélène Cixous.[9] Reversing the logic of the Zero as nothing and the One as fully present to itself as such, Plant argues that, as Zero, women can be understood to overthrow the appearance of presence upon which Man depends. Zeros in her schema are marked by neither presence nor absence, but, rather, the facilitation of everything.

Plant's updating of the image for the digital age is often intriguing. Presence and absence are configured, metaphorically or otherwise, as male and female organs of reproduction later in the book, but to start with they are confined to the bits of data upon which digital communication depends: 'Ones, whilst appearing present, depend radically on Zeros to be anything at all' (Plant 1998: 56). What characterizes Zeros, then, and paradoxically makes them 'like' women, is their capacity to be both themselves and not themselves, while Ones are destined to be alone. Further, while Ones may appear to be the origin of things, and Zeros merely a void, Zeros can be said not only to precede ones but also to generate their very possibility. As a metaphor for sexual difference, then, Zeros and Ones do the work of reversing the value inherent in the binary relation.

Again, this is particularly pertinent in a digital age when the capacity for 'rhizomatic connections' carries a positive rather than a negative significance. In her further discussion of hypertext, Plant directly connects the multiplicity of being a woman with the experience of 'surfing the web' and concludes that, 'computers have a strange affinity with women' (1998: 56). One suggestion in one plane of reason suggests another in an entirely different plane without the problem of the goal-oriented direction of being a One. Hypertext can thus be seen as a 'feminine' form, in the same way that Cixous once claimed that 'writing today is woman's' (Cixous and Clément 1987: 85). It is feminine because it is not linear and directed towards a single goal but rather multiple and multiplicitous, weaving and reweaving sense as a series of 'installations'.[10] The interplay here between 'feminine' and 'women' is as blurred as it was in the prior work of Cixous and Irigaray upon which it depends. However, there is, as there was there, a strong sense that the feminine is, at least politically, woman's. Citing the cyber feminist manifesto – 'The clitoris is a direct link to the matrix' – which appeared on a billboard in Australia in the 1990s, Plant points out that while this unsettles, it also in some senses reaffirms. As a line to the matrix, the clitoris refers also to the womb '*matrix* is the Latin term, just as *hystera* is the Greek' (998: 59) and it is difficult to avoid thinking of woman here as the hysterical effect of the unstable, organic body.

The body without organs, the cyborg, the zero network of facilitations, all are offered as radical displacements of the human in humanism's terms. Yet all are also, paradoxically, human in the sense of being knowable, present and certain to themselves in their capacity to master being. For all, the real is merely an idea and, as such, can be changed by changing the subject's idea of it. Unfortunately, what lies beyond the metaphysics, that each of these schemas seeks to transcend, is fully knowable within its terms. What is beyond, therefore, is ultimately merely a continuation of metaphysics albeit with a different set of values. This is either hopelessly utopian or downright scary, since it utterly depends on humans ideas of it. Perhaps it is both. At the very least, as a model of social transformation, it is limited. Since the relation between the human and inhuman, here, is one of replacement on the basis of human consciousness, the inhuman is ironically defused. While we can move beyond the human, we do so only by replacing the human with an inhuman which, in substituting for the human, retains all the problems of certainty in consciousness which motivated a move beyond it in the first place. In particular, as an account of gender which surpasses the cultural value of 'woman', not by engaging its impossibility but rather by asserting its possibility somewhere else, we again become bound by the terms of that somewhere else as we can conceive of it.

The issue of the inhuman

While the inhuman appears to occupy a pivotal place in defining the moment of our contemporary, it seems vital to resist any notion of it as not always already a condition of being in the world. The inhuman as that which threatens the human by assailing it from outside with everything that the human is most properly not, merely perpetuates a notion of the human founded in the certainty of presence as that which is natural and right. Within these terms, any hope of contesting the metaphysical values generated for the human is lost to an apocalyptic call to defend the real of the human in our idea of it as simply true. On the other hand, the inhuman as that which is improperly human, or as that which is *not* human and so somehow moves beyond the human leaving it trailing in its wake, is equally problematic. Simply replacing one vision of the human for another of the inhuman does not contest the process by which the values of natural right and true come to operate authoritatively in any sphere. Without addressing that process, the values of the concepts are merely retained within a different distribution of value. The inhuman, as an effect of knowledge or culture rather than nature, also ironically maintains a certainty of presence for absence even as it appears to contest it. Replacing nature with culture serves merely to replace one realm of meaning with another. Forced to choose between culture and nature, cultural criticism is forced back into the dualism of the same – either absence or presence – with no radical alterity to mark the limits of either.

While the inhuman remains the irreducible neither/nor, however, the condition of the human subject as subject of and to culture's terms, leaves open the possibility of a subversion of the subject which is constant, threatening and not limited merely to 'man's' knowledge of it. The human traced by the irreducible inhuman within, becomes a site of ambivalence, which in its everyday existence attests both to the possibility and impossibility of that existence, in terms of the meanings by which it is inscribed. Here, gender is no longer simply a problem of value addressed by alternative values, but rather a more radical impossibility which will always resist appropriation in metaphysical terms. As an intrinsically resistant impossibility, any truth for gender ascribed to the place of the human subject, regardless of its value, is always only ever the value of an imposter. Rather than fixing value to either 'this' or 'that', such a model of the human condition allows subjects to continue to resist the truth of the this and that, and thus to keep gender as an issue which is always open to debate despite our temporary ideas of it.

Desire as the metonymy of the want to be, is not possible to fulfil except in the imaginary and symbolic. Yet even there, it is never fully satisfied by the substitutes it finds. If what the subject wants is to return to the real as that which is 'always in the same place' and 'lacks nothing', then it must give up meaning as the place from which its desire and its capacity to think it are possible in the first place. In which case, we will never know that we have achieved it since we will no longer 'be there' to know anything at all. Far from the imagined pleasure of mastery, a return to the real is entirely self-destructive. I think I'll settle for its metonymic substitutions and keep the critique of meaning alive.

Conclusion

Perhaps, if cultural criticism is intent on keeping the critique of meaning alive, there can be no mastering conclusion to a work which sets out to delineate and to explore the 'key issues' pertaining to the discipline of critical and cultural theory in the third millennium. In the place of such closure, however, it may be useful to offer some remarks destined for a future as yet unanticipated.

As the practice of cultural criticism permeates the study of a variety of humanities subjects – and who knows what beyond – it seems crucial to continue to insist on at least three conditions for its operation.

In the first place, what we know of culture and the frameworks through which it is possible to analyse it never simply falls from the sky fully formed and fixed in its effect. It seems important to remember, therefore, that any ideas we encounter in our contemporary world have antecedents from which they may differ as well extend what it is possible to think and to resist in thinking. Often these can be located in extremely complex and rigorous paradigms which take some serious intellectual effort to grasp. My first insistence, then, would be that we continue to take these texts and contexts seriously. It matters, it seems to me, that we continue to engage with de Saussure, or Nietzsche, or Kant alongside Lacan, Derrida, Lyotard and Žižek, and don't simply take for granted that we have finished with the ideas offered there in the rush to move on. After all, the possibilities opened up in each new reading, and context of reading, are potentially endless.

In the second place, since, as I have argued above that the apparent effect of a paradigm of thought is not fixed for all time, it seems important also to continue to subject the thinking we do in cultural criticism to its own ongoing and perhaps ceaseless interrogation. To that end, critical and cultural theory offers ways into an engagement with cultural value, but not in exactly the same way in every instance nor in any singular way for all time. My second insistence, then, would be that we resist the urge to believe that we have arrived at the final perfected analysis which confirms that the paradigms of critical and cultural theory have enabled cultural critics somehow either to have 'got it right', or to have had the last word.

In the third place, and given all of the above, it would also seem important to suggest that while doing the hard work entailed in grasping some of the counter-intuitive concepts offered in critical writings, such as those explored in this work, we acknowledge that the goal is to resist the common sense of cultural value rather than to confirm the mastery of the reader or writer. Texts will always escape our understanding and to anticipate that is, it seems important to reiterate, to remain open to further possibilities not always either readily or obviously available at first. My third insistence, then, is that cultural criticism continues to attest to the importance of visiting and revisiting its own conceptual tools.

What all three of these insistences, I hope, suggest is that cultural criticism is necessarily hard work, that it entails intellectual rigour and scholarship even, and most especially, in the face of that which culture deems obvious, natural and true, and that it is always in process. If there is to be a last word to this work, then I should like it to be, for the time being at least, that both the effort and the pleasures involved in the practice of cultural criticism as it has been suggested here should not be underestimated.

Glossary

alterity, used in place of 'otherness' to emphasize a sense of difference as separation.

aporias, in Derrida's work, an insoluble paradox.

Cartesian, refers to the mind–body dualism which grounds being in thinking. Here thinking is understood to take precedence over being by defining it. The antecedent for this is generally acknowledged to be René Descartes' formulation 'I think, therefore, I am' (*The Fourth Discourse on the Method of Rightly Conducting Reason and Reaching the Truth in the Sciences*, 1637).

desire, is the perpetual effect in the subject of the movement of signification. Humans become **subjects** by giving up the raw state of being for the promise of representation within meaning. Lacan likens this process to being robbed by a highwayman who demands 'your money or your life' – you can have one or the other, but you cannot have both (1991: 146). While meaning offers the possibility of intelligibility, however, it does so only in reference to its own terms and conditions. Arriving from being into a place inscribed in meaning, then, the subject is lost like an object in the defiles of **signification** as the continual process of difference and deferral. The subject thus constituted is doubly lacking – it has forsaken being and in the process become subject to the impossibility of presence in the movement that signification is. Desire, in these terms, is the futile attempt to overcome the lack which founds subjectivity. As such, it is destined to remain unfulfilled since any substitute for the original loss is ironically possible only within meanings terms. The paradox is that meaning both initiates desire and makes it impossible to fulfil.

dialectical materialism, taking the dialectic from Hegel and materialism from Marx, the phrase designates the concept of movement, or change, through the gradual emergence of contradictions within the structures of social organization (usually economic).

disavowal, the process by which the **subject** protects the **ego** from anything which threatens its undoing.

ego, the sense of self acquired by subjects within the terms of culture which serves to define the **subject** to itself (see **imaginary**).

estrangement, usually designates a form of separation within the same. In these terms, estrangement marks the play of the other within the same which keeps the same from being fully itself.

humanistic, the doctrine that places the human at the centre of knowledge, as both originator of, and destination for knowledge (see **Cartesian**).

imaginary, one of Lacan's three orders with the **symbolic** and real, the imaginary is bound to both. In the context of the three registers, it designates the imagined image of the subject to itself and all that sustains that subject in that image.

imago, the identity of the subject **misrecognized** in the image of itself within the **imaginary**.

immanentism, the belief that self is fully present within itself and therefore lacking nothing. Immanentism is usually an assumed priority of self as the ground and guarantee of knowledge.

metaphysics, the system within which knowledge is constituted and thus the 'world' (*physics*) is rendered intelligible. **Western metaphysics** designates the particularities of the system of intelligibility in the West, and thus indicates that metaphysics is not truth.

misrecognition, the apparent recognition of self in the image offered by culture. This is a misrecognition precisely because, as culture, the image offered is exterior to the **subject**, yet comes to seem as if it is unique to that subject.

other, designates that which is not the same. This can be the symbolic as Other to the **subject** and other people as not the same as self. Lacan distinguishes the two as big other (capital O) and little other (lower case o).

petit objet a, is the object of desire which will never be attained but which the subject is motivated endlessly to seek. The object is 'a' from the French 'autre' and so designates that which is not present to the subject since it is **other**.

phallogocentrism, signifies the value structure of **Western metaphysics** by combining *phal* (the signifier of power usually imagined to belong to men in patriarchy), *logos* (the centrality of the word as though meaning were present there), and *centrism* (as the centrality of the two). For Lacan, the phal, or phallus, is an important signifier of power in the social order but, as signifier, does not belong to any subject man or woman.

points de capiton, these are the points within the movement of signification where that movement appears temporarily to be anchored, or secure.

poststructuralist, delineates the theoretical terrain that takes off from the implications of Saussure's theory of language as a system of difference and deferral producing rather than simply describing meaning.

presence/absence, a dualism of **Western metaphysics** which appears to designate the certainty of something and nothing. For Derrida, that apparent certainty is undermined in the structure that produces it, since both terms are interdependent. Presence is everything that absence is not and vice versa, therefore, presence contains the **trace** of absence and absence the trace of presence. As a result, neither is either fully present or absent.

sign, in Saussure's work, which posits language as a system of signs, the sign is the associative total of the signifier and signified (for further exploration of the *concept* of the sign, see Chapter 1).

signification, the meaning, acknowledged culturally, of a particular sign or chain of **signs**.

signify, the process of making meaning in Saussure's terms.

subject, designates the condition of being in meaning as both subject of and to meaning. As such, it marks the shift in thinking away from the natural self which is presumed to be simply 'there', to the notion of self as an effect of the confluence of imaginary, symbolic and real.

sublimation, the redirection of anything which threatens the **ego**, in its image of self, into something less threatening. This can carry the **trace** of the real, as instinct say, which is deflected into something safer within the terms of meaning.

superego, 'over-I', the superego is the function of regulating the maintenance of the **ego** in the direction of social value.

symbolic, the order of meaning as a system of signification in Lacan. As such, it designates the realm of signifying structures as systematic and self-referential, but also as those structures are held in the inevitable confluence of the three orders: **imaginary**, symbolic and real.

textuality, the condition of **signification** as it is made into a particular *form*.

Thing, the impossible object sought by the **subject** in order to make good the lack which founds it. Thing is, therefore, impossible to define and always elusive. In Lacan's later work, Thing gets transcribed into ***petit objet a***.

trace, the play of the **other** within the self-same. The trace is that which keeps something from being itself by foregrounding the dependence of that something on that which is other to it.

Übermensch, 'overman' in Nietzsche, signifies an atheistic ideal of man as creator of his own life. The *Übermensch* resists existing cultural value, especially morality, by returning to the affirmative power of earthly existence as raw unstructured nature.

uncanny, marks that feeling of strangeness within the subject that is both familiar and yet unnervingly unfamiliar, odd and somehow out of joint.

Notes

Chapter 1 Textuality and signification

1. Oasis is a Manchester band principally formed around two brothers, Noel and Liam Gallagher. The brothers grew up on a council estate in the Manchester district of Burnage. The song 'Wonderwall' comes from their album *(What's the Story) Morning Glory?* (1995).
2. For a more detailed account of the work of Saussure, see Jonathan Culler (1990).
3. The formulation 'human animals' is awkward. It is used here to distinguish the condition of being human, and therefore capable of signifying in ways which animals are not, but at the same time to mark a difference to 'the subject' which becomes subject to language in the act of acquiring that language.
4. The image of cutting here echoes a kind of violence which is resonant throughout Saussure's account of what language does.
5. Again, the force of the term 'forge' is resonant of Saussure's continuing metaphor of the 'violence' which language performs.
6. The essay 'Freud and the Scene of Writing' also provides some interesting material in relation to debates about artificial intelligence as machinic thinking.
7. Derrida became frustrated by the outrage generated by this statement based on a reading of it as signalling that the text is all there is. In order to discourage his phrase from being used to justify a reading of texts as reducible merely to 'the words on the page' as though they were self-contained, he redrafted his earlier statement. Even Derrida, it would seem, suffers the vagaries of signification.
8. This does, and should, have implications for one avenue of critical and cultural thinking currently conducted under the sign 'trauma studies'.
9. The concept of the other is one with specific parameters within, in the critical and cultural theory expounded here. As such, it can carry a range of signification from language and culture to other people, even difference. All of these significations will be addressed in context in the different chapters of this book, but in particular in Chapter 4 on Alterity.
10. This reading of the relation of self-image to the gaze of the other is expounded in Chapter 4 on Alterity.

Chapter 2 Aesthetics

1 The term 'thing-in-itself' is Kant's and first appeared in *Prolegomena to Any Future Metaphysics* ([1783] 1986).

2 Immanuel Kant (1724–1804) was a German Enlightenment philosopher writing in the eighteenth and early nineteenth centuries.

3 The term 'man' was used unproblematically in philosophy as elsewhere for quite some time. However, since it generates a sexist meaning by excluding 'women' semantically and ideologically, it has fallen into disrepute as a sign pertaining to human kind. I shall use the term in this aspect of the discussion of the sublime as any rendition of it in its ideological terms would prove awkward to the argument pursued. I shall take it that, having noted the error, the reader will assume that the term appears here 'under erasure'.

4 The notion of sense as a visceral knowledge is also developed by the philosophical/psychoanalytic writing duo of Gilles Deleuze and Félix Guattari. For further reference, see *Cinema 1: The Movement Image* (2005a), and *Cinema 2: The Time Image* (2005b).

5 For Kant, both 'ways of knowing' were a means by which to develop the morality of 'man', which he later expounded in *Groundwork of the Metaphysics of Morals* ([1785] 2002).

6 To say that Lyotard is a 'postmodern philosopher' is somewhat erroneous, since he theorized the postmodern. A certain caution should be exercised in designating anything as simply 'postmodern' in critical and cultural theory today. Here the term is used to signify philosophy as it is constituted specifically in Lyotard's analysis of the postmodern condition.

7 See Jean-François Lyotard, *The Postmodern Condition: A Report on Knowledge* (2001).

8 'The state of aesthetics' is a term used by Lyotard to signify the debate today and appears in the title of one of his key essays, 'After the Sublime, the State of Aesthetics' in *The Inhuman: Reflections on Time* (1993).

9 For further elaboration of this position, see Fredric Jameson, *Postmodernism, or the Cultural Logic of Late Capitalism* (1991).

10 In *The Postmodern Condition* (2001), Lyotard theorizes the operation of the grand narratives of legitimation via Wittgenstein's notion of language as game. The analysis that ensues focuses on how these narratives work – the rules of the game by which each is played. In this sense, Lyotard's analysis of grand narratives shares some similarities with the analysis of signification addressed in Chapter 1.

11 'Abyss' suggests a limitless nothingness, but also carries with it a sense of despair.

12 Here 'matter' signifies the materiality of sound. It still carries the sense of matter as signification.

13 A distinction must be drawn here between two senses of matter for Lyotard. In the first, as signification, matter can be shown to be immaterial. In the second, as the organic matter of human being, any immateriality is deadly. This death of the matter of the subject, as opposed to its signification, is explored more fully in another essay from *The Inhuman* (1993) in which Lyotard argues strongly for retaining this second sense. This essay, 'Can Thought Go On Without a Body?' is addressed in this book in Chapter 5, which explores conceptualizations of the real.

14 Of particular note in this regard is Slavoj Žižek's account of '9/11' in *Welcome to the Desert of the Real* (2002).

15 Another philosopher who has had trouble within the establishment of philosophy, as a result of putting language on its agenda, is Jacques Derrida. The decision, by Cambridge University in 1993, to award Derrida an honorary doctorate, caused great controversy within the philosophy department whose notion of a 'Cambridge philosophy' did not include analyses of language as a proper site of inquiry.

16 The German term *Übermensch* can be translated into English as 'overman'. For Nietzsche, it signifies a mode of existence in which the life force is not curtailed by the weaknesses of culture.

17 Importantly, Nietzsche is not simply arguing here that all truth is relative and, therefore, that there can never be anything which grounds value. He merely suggests that truth is always invested by a value it disavows. It is, therefore, never true.

18 The similarities with Samuel Taylor Coleridge's figure of the ancient mariner, in the poem by that name, are striking in this passage.

19 This is apparent throughout Nietzsche's work, but particularly evident in his writings on the overman, democracy and atheism.

20 One particularly strange example of this can be found in websites that reproduce images of the moment of impact of each of the planes on the World Trade Center in New York on September 11, 2001. Clouds of smoke are read as signs of prophetic meaning – most usually of God's wrath, or bin Laden's omnipotent evil.

21 Freud's essay on 'The Uncanny' carries a discussion of the term '*unheimlich*' in several different languages. In the Penguin Freud Library volume *Art and Literature* (1990), this can be found on pages 341–7.

Chapter 3 Ethics

1 'Man made language' is a term coined by the feminist writer Dale Spender in the book of the same name. Here she argues that women are in part oppressed by the masculine nature of language, made by men.

The argument about the nineteenth-century novel and about painting as bourgeois art forms, is made in Marxist criticism on the basis that, *as forms*, both are conservative of the status quo. The novel, because it is a form of classical realism which, does nothing to question dominant perceptions of the world as simply 'there'; painting because it employs similar means of representation.

For more on the concept of photography as fetishism, particularly in relation to race, gender and sexuality, see Kobena Mercer's essay 'Reading racial fetishism: the photographs of Robert Mapplethorpe', in *Welcome to the Jungle: New Positions in Black Cultural Studies* (1994).

2 Two of the most popular television representations of life in New York – itself the cosmopolitan capital of the USA – are currently *Friends* and *Sex and the City*. Both portray an idea of America through two different sets of friendship groups, neither of which includes Black Americans, Asian Americans or Latin American Americans.

3 Antonio Gramsci (1891–1937) was an Italian Marxist who was imprisoned by the fascist authorities, in Italy, in 1926. From his prison cell he wrote a series of theoretical accounts of power in culture and society. These have subsequently been collated and published. One example is the edition published by Routledge as *Prison Notebooks: Selections* (1973).

4 For Gramsci, the term 'subaltern' signified those people who were dominated by others in a hierarchy of power. The subaltern was then the figure of the powerless. The term 'subaltern' comes from military discourse to indicate rank.

5 Spivak first used the term 'strategic essentialism' in writing about the work of the subaltern studies group in volume 4 of *Subaltern Studies: Writings on South Asian History and Society* (1985).

6 The phrase 'ways out' echoes that made famous by the French feminist writer Hélène Cixous, in her essay 'Sorties' (1986). Here, Cixous seeks ways out of the single, goal-orientated, focus of the movement of signification as she sees it in masculinist terms. Her analysis in the essay is partly derived from Lacan and partly from Derrida, and begins with a deconstruction of what she sees as the gendered binaries that sustain Western metaphysics.

7 Spivak mobilizes the term 'catachrestic' in order to expound her strategy of using terms which she knows to be false. By making mistakes with concepts, she suggests that we can expunge them of their usual implications. Catachresis signifies an incorrect use of words.

8 In *The Four Fundamental Concepts of Psychoanalysis* (1991), Lacan jokes that the move from being into meaning, is like the choice offered by the highwayman who asks you to choose 'Your money or your life!' You can have one or the other, but you can't have both.

9 Lacan remarks that this 'I' is 'symbolized in dreams as a fortress' (2003: 5).

10 The superego here, is that which Freud writes as 'I', 'it' and 'over-I' in *The Ego and the Id* ([1923] 2001b). A precise and useful discussion of this can be found in Antony Easthope's *The Unconscious* (1999).

11 Freud's 'Wo es war, soll Ich werden' has been translated differently in different contexts. It appears in English as 'Where it was, I shall come to be,' 'Where it was, there ego shall be'. The Slovenian critic Slavoj Žižek translates it as, 'Where it was, I shall come into being' and uses this translation to frame the series of publications he edits for Verso under the title 'Wo ES WAR'.

12 'Live 8' was a live music event which took place in Hyde Park, London, and simultaneously at a number of venues around the world in June 2005. Its purpose was to raise funds for starving peoples in Africa and at the same time to raise awareness about the causes and effects of poverty there. It was called 'Live 8' in part as a reference to concerts which had taken place before as 'Live Aid' and 'Band Aid' with similar purposes. It was also a reference to the G8 summit of world leaders which was taking place in Edinburgh in the week following the concert in Hyde Park.

13 BBC World Service reported on 6 July 2005 on the profits made by the already wealthy musicians who took part, giving statistics on record sales increased since the concert took place. In some cases, music which hadn't sold well in previous years suddenly rocketed in sales once the concert was broadcast live.

14 'Hope' is a term Derrida uses in the dialogues with Jürgen Habermas published as *Philosophy in a Time of Terror*. See Borradori (2003). Hope resonates with the possibility of possibilities.

15 The story of Abraham is told in the Bible in Genesis 22:1–19.

Chapter 4 Alterity

1 The 'fetish' for Freud is that which, as an object, is overvalued. The fetish of difference in this respect refers to the overvaluation of the specificities of cultural differences outside of any concept of what difference, conceptually, is and does. An argument to this effect is made about a range of cultural work by Antony Easthope in his book *Privileging Difference* (2002).

2 On 11 September 2001, I re-found the ticket that had admitted me to the World Trade Center in New York City the previous year. All that was written there was the following phrase, 'Welcome to the top of the world'. I was struck by the imperialism of its announcement.

3 The etymology of the word 'interest' is in itself interesting. Once a sign signifying simply money, following the Industrial Revolution in Europe it took on the signification of self. A Marxist reading of the individualization of self in capitalism is not far from its horizon.

4 For Lacan, psychosis is in part marked by a 'dislocation' that occurs for the subject in the relation to the signifier. Lacan's more detailed thinking on psychosis can be found in *The Psychoses, 1955–1956* (1993).

5 'Dominant specularity' is a term used within film theory to signify the relation established between the film and spectator. An analysis of the

consequences of this relation can be found in Colin MacCabe's essay 'Realism and Cinema: Notes on Some Brechtian Theses' (1985).

6 A slippage of terminology occurs in this section between the ego-Ideal and Ideal I. Since the mirror stage occurs prior to the acquisition of language, the ego-Ideal signifies the initial formation of an infant's sense of itself, and the Ideal I the formalization of that in language.

7 The term 'ethnic cleansing' circulates in culture today as signifying the violent expulsion of peoples within a nation who are deemed not to belong. In the Balkan states and in Africa, this has included mass killing and burial which is illegal under international law. In the partition of India by the British in 1947, all Muslims living in India were forced to relocate to what became Pakistan as a result of the partition of the country of India. There are actually two parts to Pakistan – Pakistan (which is the region bordering Afghanistan in the West) and East Pakistan (which includes Bangladesh). Partition entailed often violent clashes between Muslims and Hindus, and long arduous journeys for people who lost everything they had.

8 The British government has produced a 'Citizenship Guide' for immigrants which is supposed to guide readers 'along the journey to citizenship'. However, as was reported in *The Guardian* newspaper by Lee Glendinning on 29 April 2006, the guide gets some basic details of British history wrong. Among many glaring errors, the booklet, entitled *Life in the United Kingdom: A Journey to Citizenship*, confuses the United Kingdom with Great Britain (the UK includes Northern Ireland, the Channel Islands and the Isle of Man; Great Britain is made up of England, Wales and Scotland) and it puts Hadrian's Wall in Scotland (it's in England).

9 'May '68' signifies the general strike across France in 1968, which seemed to threaten revolution.

10 Althusser is not quite so resolute about there being no position outside of ideology. While his stance that ideology constitutes subjects and is therefore not merely thrust upon them as a form of false consciousness, marks his difference from previous Marxist models, he does reserve a place outside of ideology for what he terms 'science'. This allows him to be able to explain the function and effect of ideology without being subject to its fantasy. This proved problematic, and Marxist thinkers have gradually extended Althusser's model of ideology to the domain of science. Whether Marxism has quite shaken off the aura of seeing the real conditions of man's existence, however, is another matter.

11 The concept of 'hybridity' is discussed by Bhabha in *The Location of Culture* (1995).

12 While the discussion of Lévinas here focuses on his contribution to the subject–other relation, a great deal of what he writes about the problems of alterity pertains to philosophy as a discipline and to the branch of ontology in particular. Lévinas, like Derrida, criticizes Western philosophy for its dependence on an expulsion of its own other in order to be what it is. This other

for Lévinas is the face-to-face encounter between subjects which philosophy cannot grasp.

Chapter 5 The real

1 Marx's principle of false consciousness is derived from his economic model of social organization. Here the means and mode of production (the economic base) give rise to a superstructure (consciousness as ideology) in which the reproduction of the base is secured by ideas which cover over the exploitation of the working class within the system. Actually, although this idea is widely attributed to Karl Marx (it's one of the 'classical' Marxist principles), it comes from a text jointly authored with Frederick Engels – *The German Ideology* (1846). In that text, they write that

> The ideas of the ruling class are in every epoch the ruling ideas: i.e. the class which is the ruling *material* force of society is at the same time its ruling intellectual force . . . The ruling ideas are nothing more than the ideal expression of the dominant material relations, the dominant material relations grasped as ideas.
>
> (Easthope and McGowan, 2004: 39)

The active intellectual class in these terms is the conscious class and the working class, the class upon whom that consciousness is foisted.

Like Guattari in the writing duo Deleuze and Guattari, it seems it is Engels' fate to be overlooked.

2 Andy Warhol's artistic technique is an interesting one. Taking photographs, he then processed them first by silk screening over the photographic image and then by painting over that. Often the silk screening was repeated in different colours and the repetition of the image did not entirely coincide with the previous versions. For some reason, his status as an artist was, and is still, contested.

3 Baudrillard's depiction of the cultural critic as terrorist can sound like that of Derrida's 'vigilant critique' explored in the preceding chapter. However, one vital difference between the two is the mode of writing each employs. For Derrida, the rigorous gesture is the one which inhabits the texts of others in order to minutely scrutinize the assumptions and implications that may previously have gone unnoticed there and so to produce a slightly different set of possibilities while acknowledging a 'debt'. For Baudrillard, the point is always to write something 'new' and so to 'obfuscate' by entirely re- circulating cultural objects. Where Derrida might suggest there's more to be thought about a text already in circulation, Baudrillard goes for the explosion

of all ideas that you might know where it is you're going, leaving nothing but ruin in his wake. Well, that's the idea anyway . . .

4 The negation of the negation is a well-known, and well argued, aspect of philosophical thinking. Žižek stages his own long discussion of the principle of the negation of negation in his work *The Ticklish Subject* (2000).

5 The concept of the 'inter-dit' as the 'inter-said' is one that can be found in Lacan's 'Subversion of the subject and the dialectic of desire', which is the final essay in the *Écrits*. Here Lacan differentiates the inter-dit from the intra-dit in order to demonstrate his own theory of the 'fading' of the subject as it passes through signification.

6 The analysis of inter-ethnic conflict includes analyses of the redrawing of boundaries in the Balkan states of Europe. In particular, Žižek has an interest in the breakup of Yugoslavia, and this pervades his analyses of culture. For a 'quick fix', Žižek's article 'Eastern Europe's Republics of Gilead' in *New Left Review* (1990) is worth a look.

7 The notion of the 'new' millennium and the worst of *fin-de-siècle* pronouncements to which it gave rise, is something that Žižek, as well as others, have rightly criticized. Every era believes itself to be unique and seems compelled to demonstrate this most strongly in showing how new eras, new millennia, bring paradigm shifting change. The concept of the epoch itself perhaps needs some more rigorous work.

8 See Catherine Belsey's *Culture and the Real* (2005) and Antony Easthope's *Privileging Difference* (2002). For Lacan on the idealism of Hegel, and why Lacan is not, therefore, a Hegelian, see his own essay, 'The Subversion of the Subject and the Dialectic of Desire in the Freudian Unconscious' (2003: 323–58).

Chapter 6 The inhuman

1 As I write this chapter, American scientists have succeeded for the first time in growing a human bladder from stem cells taken from a human. That bladder can, in principle, now be implanted back into that same human in order to replace a 'faulty' organic original. This does not carry the usual possibilities of rejection since it is an exact tissue match. Indeed, it is the *same* tissue.

2 Britain has been bombarded in the last five years by media headlines which tag the name of Mary Shelley's fictional doctor to anything from food, which contains genetically modified ingredients ('Frankenstinean food'), to face transplants carried out in France. This might suggest a limit to the human imagination.

3 For the British writer D.H. Lawrence, the 'proper' as it is delineated here was attached very powerfully to the signifier of gender and gendered relations. While *Lady Chatterley's Lover* opens with a dystopian vision of civilization on the brink of destruction, it becomes apparent in the course of the narrative

that this is because 'proper value' has been put out of joint. If only the women 'u'd begin to be women,' then the men could 'properly be men'. 'It's because th' men aren't men, that th' women have to be' (1928: 222).

4 Fukuyama's vision of the possible future he depicts in this book is rhetorically apocalyptic. Since the future is yet to come, the job of delineating the dangers that ensue from biotechnology is to urge the avoidance of the possibility of succumbing to those dangers unthinkingly.

5 Here Derrida is re-reading Heidegger's ontological account of being as both Being and being-in-the-world. Hence the distinction between the capital B and the lower case b.

6 In his essay on *Lyotard and the Inhuman* (2001), Stuart Sim suggests that Lyotard succumbs to a form of humanism. Having drawn a distinction himself between good forms and bad forms of humanism, this is offered by Sim as a good, if unacknowledged, thing in Lyotard's work. I find no evidence of any sort of humanism, nostalgic or otherwise, in Lyotard's account here.

7 This paradoxical location of the human as a displacement in the movement of an impossible desire is elaborated in relation to cinema in the article, 'Oedipal androids: desire and the human in the third millennium' (McGowan 2006).

8 Lacan consistently states that sexual difference is one of the founding differences in Western metaphysics. However, this is not the same as suggesting that it is somehow simply real. Rather, 'masculine' and 'feminine' are, for Lacan, positions within the symbolic.

9 See, for example, the discussion of Cixous' account of the feminine as heterogeneity in *The Newly Born Woman* (Cixous and Clément 1987).

10 This weaving of a series of installations has resonances with Plant's earlier work on the Situationist movement in Europe. See Plant (1992).

Bibliography

Adorno, Theodor W. (1967) *PRISMS: Cultural Criticism and Society: Spengler, Huxley, Kafka, Proust, Schoenberg, Jazz, etc.*, trans. Samuel Weber and Shierry Weber. London: Neville Spearman.

Adorno, Theodor W. (1990) *Negative Dialectics*, trans. London and New York, NY: E.B. Ashton.

Althusser, Louis (1971) *Lenin and Philosophy*, trans. Ben Brewster. London: Verso.

Barthes, Roland (1990) *Image-Music-Text*, trans. Stephen Heath. London: Fontana.

Baudrillard, Jean (1983) *Simulations*, trans. Paul Foss *et al.* New York, NY: Semiotext(e).

Baudrillard, Jean (1993) *Symbolic Exchange and Death*, trans. Iain Hamilton Grant. London: Sage.

Baudrillard, Jean (1995) *The Gulf War Did Not Take Place*, trans. Paul Patton. Sydney: Power Publications.

Baudrillard, Jean (1996) *The Perfect Crime*, trans. Chris Turner. London: Verso.

Baudrillard, Jean (2002) *The Spirit of Terrorism*, trans. Chris Turner. London: Verso.

Belsey, Catherine (2005) *Culture and the Real: Theorizing Cultural Criticism*. London: Routledge.

Benjamin, Walter (1999) *Illuminations*, trans. Harry Zorn. London: Pimlico.

Bhabha, Homi K. (1995) *The Location of Culture*. London: Routledge.

Borradori, Giovanna (2003) *Philosophy in a Time of Terror: Dialogues with Jürgen Habermas and Jacques Derrida*. Chicago, IL: University of Chicago Press.

Brewster, Scott *et al.* (eds) (2000) *Inhuman Reflections: Thinking the Limits of the Human*. Manchester: Manchester University Press.

Carroll, Lewis (2000) *The Annotated Alice*, ed. Martin Gardner. London: Penguin.

Cixous, Hélène (1986) 'Sorties', in Hélène Cixous and Catherine Clément (eds) *The Newly Born Woman*, trans. Betsy Wing. Manchester: Manchester University Press.

Cixous, Hélène and Clément, Catherine (1987) *The Newly Born Woman*, trans. Betsy Wing. Manchester: Manchester University Press.

Coggeshall, Ralph of (2006) *Chronicles*. Cited in the BBC Radio Four programme *The Long View* aired on 4 April.

Conrad, Joseph (1994) *Heart of Darkness*. London: Penguin.

Culler, Jonathan (1990) *Saussure*. London: Fontana.

Deleuze, Gilles and Guattari, Félix (2003) *What Is Philosophy?* trans. Graham Burchell and Hugh Tomlinson. London: Verso.

Deleuze, Gilles and Guattari, Félix (2004a) *Anti-Oedipus: Capitalism and*

Schizophrenia, trans. Robert Hurley, Mark Seem and Helen R. Lane. London: Continuum.

Deleuze, Gilles and Guattari, Félix (2004b) *A Thousand Plateaus: Capitalism and Schizophrenia*, trans. Brian Massumi. London: Continuum.

Deleuze, Gilles and Guattari, Félix (2005a) *Cinema 1: The Movement Image*. London: Continuum.

Deleuze, Gilles and Guattari, Félix (2005b) *Cinema 2: The Time Image*. London: Continuum.

Derrida, Jacques (1973) *Speech, Phenomena and Other Essays on Husserl's Theory of Signs*, trans. David B. Allison. Evanston, IL: Northwestern University Press.

Derrida, Jacques (1976) *Of Grammatology*, trans. Gayatri Chakravorty Spivak. Baltimore, MD: Johns Hopkins University Press.

Derrida, Jacques (1988) *Limited Inc*, trans. Samuel Weber. Evanston, IL: Northwestern University Press.

Derrida, Jacques (1994) *Given Time: 1. Counterfeit Money*, trans Peggy Kamuf. Chicago, IL: University of Chicago Press.

Derrida, Jacques (1996) *The Gift of Death*, trans. David Wills. Chicago, IL: University of Chicago Press.

Derrida, Jacques (2004a) *Writing and Difference*, trans Alan Bass. London: Routledge.

Derrida, Jacques (2004b) *For What Tomorrow ... A Dialogue*, with Elisabeth Roudinesco, trans. Jeff Fort. Stanford, CA: Stanford University Press.

Easthope, Antony (1999) *The Unconscious*. London: Routledge.

Easthope, Antony (2002) *Privileging Difference*, ed. Catherine Belsey. Basingstoke: Palgrave.

Easthope, Antony and McGowan, Kate (eds) (2004) *A Critical and Cultural Theory Reader*, (2nd edn.). Maidenhead: Open University Press.

Ethics and aesthetics, http://www.umich.edu/~eng499/concepts/ethics.html accessed 2005.

Fanon, Frantz (1991) *Black Skin, White Masks*, trans. Charles Lam Markham. London: Pluto Press.

Freud, Sigmund (1900) *The Standard Edition of the Complete Psychological Works of Sigmund Freud*, vol. v: *The Interpretation of Dreams*, ed. James Strachey. London: Hogarth Press.

Freud, Sigmund (1974) *The Standard Edition of the Complete Psychological Works of Sigmund Freud*, vol. xiv: *Papers on Metapsychology*, ed. James Strachey. London: Hogarth Press.

Freud, Sigmund (1990) *Art and Literature*, trans. Alix Strachey, The Penguin Freud Library, vol. 14. London: Penguin Books.

Freud, Sigmund (2001a) *Group Psychology and the Analysis of the Ego*, in *The Complete Psychological Works of Sigmund Freud*, vol. 18, ed. James Strachey. New York, NY: Vintage Publications.

Freud, Sigmund ([1923] 2001b) *The Complete Psychological Works of Sigmund Freud*, vol. 19: *'The Ego and the Id' and Other Works,* ed. James Strachey. New York, NY: Vintage Publications.

Fukuyama, Francis (2003) *Our Posthuman Future: Consequences of the Biotechnology Revolution*. London: Profile Books.

Gramsci, Antonio (1973) *Prison Notebooks: Selections*, ed. Geoffrey Nowell-Smith. London: Routledge.

Guardian, the (2005) 'Man used electric underpants to fake heart attack.' 5 July 2005.

Hall, Stuart (1992) 'What is this 'Black' in Black Popular Culture?' in Gina Dent (ed.) *Black Popular Culture*. Seattle, MA: Bay Press.

Haraway, Donna J. (1991) *Simians, Cyborgs, and Women: The Reinvention of Nature*. London: Free Association Books.

Hegel, G.W.F. (1993) *Introductory Lectures on Aesthetics*, trans. Bernard Bosenquet. London: Penguin.

Husserl, Edmund (1995) *Cartesian Meditations: An Introduction to Phenomenology*. trans. Dorian Cairns. Dordrecht: Kluwer Academic.

Jameson, Fredric (1991) *Postmodernism, or the Cultural Logic of Late Capitalism*. Durham, NC: Duke University Press.

Joyce, James (1982) *Ulysses*. London: Penguin.

Kant, Immanuel ([1783] 1986) *Prolegomena to Any Future Metaphysics That Will Be Able to Come Forward as Science,* trans. P. Carus. Chicago, IL: Open Court Publishing Company.

Kant, Immanuel (1987) *Critique of Judgment*, trans. Werner S. Pluhar. Indianapolis, IN: Hackett.

Kant, Immanuel (1990) *Critique of Pure Reason*, trans. Norman Kemp Smith. London: Macmillan.

Kant, Immanuel ([1785] 2002) *Groundwork of the Metaphysics of Morals*, trans Mary Gregor. Cambridge: Cambridge University Press.

Lacan, Jacques (1991) *The Four Fundamental Concepts of Psychoanalysis*, trans. Alan Sheridan. London: Penguin Books.

Lacan, Jacques (1993) *The Psychoses: The Seminar of Jacques Lacan Book III, 1955–56,* trans. Russell Grigg. London: Routledge.

Lacan, Jacques (1999) *The Ethics of Psychoanalysis, 1959–60: The Seminar of Jacques Lacan Book VII*, trans. Dennis Porter. London: Routledge.

Lacan, Jacques (2003) *Écrits: A Selection*, trans. Alan Sheridan. London: Routledge.

Lawrence, D.H. (1928) *Lady Chatterley's Lover*. London: Penguin.

Lévinas, Emmanuel (1998) *Entre Nous: Thinking-of-the-Other*, trans. Michael B. Smith and Barbara Harshav. New York, NY: Columbia University Press.

Lévinas, Emmanuel ([1961] 2003) *Totality and Infinity: An Essay on Exteriority*, trans. Alphonso Lingis. Pittsburgh, PA: Duquesne University Press.

Lyotard, Jean-François (1993) *The Inhuman: Reflections on Time,* trans. Geoffrey Bennington and Rachel Bowlby. Cambridge: Polity Press.

Lyotard, Jean-François (1994) *Lessons on the Analytic of the Sublime*, trans. Elizabeth Rottenberg. Stanford, CA: Stanford University Press.

Lyotard, Jean-François (1998) *The Assassination of Experience in Painting – Monery*, trans. Rachel Bowlby. London: Black Dog.

Lyotard, Jean-François (2001) *The Postmodern Condition: A Report on Knowledge*, trans. Geoff Bennington and Brian Massumi. Manchester: Manchester University Press.

MacCabe, Colin (1985) *Theoretical Essays*. Manchester: Manchester University Press.

McGowan, Kate (2006) 'Oedipal androids: desire and the human in the third millennium', *Technoetic Arts: A Journal of Speculative Research*, 4(1): 39–54.

Mercer, Kobena (1994) 'Reading racial fetishism: the photographs of Robert Mapplethorpe,' in *Welcome to the Jungle: New Positions in Black Cultural Studies*. London: Routledge.

Monk, Daniel (2002) *An Aesthetic Occupation: The Immediacy of Architecture and the Palestine Conflict*. Durham, NC: Duke University Press.

Nelson, Cary *et al.*, (eds) (1988) *Marxism and the Interpretation of Culture*. London: Palgrave Macmillan.

Nietzsche, Friedrich (1954) *The Portable Nietzsche*, trans. Walter Kaufman. New York, NY: Viking Press.

Nietzsche, Friedrich (1974) *The Gay Science*, trans. Walter Kaufmann. New York, NY: Vintage Books.

Nietzsche, Friedrich (1990) *Beyond Good and Evil: Prelude to a Philosophy of the Future*, trans. R.J. Hollingdale. London: Penguin.

Nietzsche, Friedrich (1995) *The Birth of Tragedy*, trans. Clifton P. Fadiman. New York, NY: Dover Publications, Inc.

Nietzsche, Friedrich (2003) *Thus Spake Zarathustra*, trans. Thomas Wayne. New York, NY: Algora Publishers .

Plant, Sadie (1992) *The Most Radical Gesture: Situationist International in a Postmodern Age*. London: Routledge.

Plant, Sadie (1998) *Zeros and Ones: Digital Women and New Technoculture*. London: Fourth Estate.

Rattansi, Ali and Westwood, Sally (eds) (1994) *Racism, Modernity and Identity: On the Western Front*. London: Polity Press.

Said, Edward (1985) *Orientalism*. London: Pantheon Books.

Saussure, Ferdinand de (1966) *Course in General Linguistics*, trans. Wade Baskin. New York, NY: McGraw-Hill.

Sim, Stuart (2001) *Lyotard and the Inhuman*. London: Icon Books.

Spender, Dale (1985) *Man-made Language*. London: Routledge.

Spivak, Gayatri Chakravorty (1985) 'Subaltern studies: deconstructing historiography' in *Subaltern Studies: Writings on South Asian History and Society*, vol.4. Oxford: Oxford University Press.

Spivak, Gayatri Chakravorty (1988) 'Can the subaltern speak?' in Cary Nelson *et al.* (eds) *Marxism and the Interpretation of Culture*. London: Palgrave Macmillan.

Spivak, Gayatri Chakravorty (1990) *The Post-colonial Critic: Interviews, Strategies, Dialogues*. London: Routledge.

Stanford Encyclopedia of Philosophy (2005) http://plato.standford.edu/entries/feminism-ethics/ accessed September 2005.

Stockhausen, Karlheinz (2001) Cited in 'uncertain reality' in *Governing Terrorism: The Media and 9/11* at http://c250.columbia.edu/dkv/eseminars/ accessed 19 April 2006.

Tate, Shirley Anne (2005). *Black Skins, Black Masks: Hybridity-Dialogism-Performativity*. Aldershot: Ashgate.

Tzara, Tristan (1992) *Seven Dada Manifestos and Lampisteries*, trans. Barbara Wright. London: Calder Publications.

Werbner, Pnina (1998) 'The dialectics of cultural hybridity', in Pnina Werbner and Tariq Modood, eds. *Debating Cultural Hybridity: Multi-Cultural Identities and the Politics of Racism*. London: Zed Books.

Žižek, Slavoj (1990) 'Eastern Europe's Republic of Gillead,' *New Left Review* 183: 50–63.

Žižek, Slavoj (1991) *For They Know Not What They Do: Enjoyment as a Political Factor*. London: Verso.

Žižek, Slavoj (1999) *The Sublime Object of Ideology*. London: Verso.

Žižek, Slavoj (2000) *The Ticklish Subject: The Absent Centre of Political Ontology*. London: Verso.

Žižek, Slavoj (2001) *Enjoy Your Symptom: Jacques Lacan in Hollywood and Out*. 2nd edn. London: Routledge.

Žižek, Slavoj (2002) *Welcome to the Desert of the Real*. London: Verso.

Žižek, Slavoj (2005) *Interrogating the Real*. London: Continuum.

Index